# *Dancing with the Unknown*

**FEELINGS and**

**Everyday MIND and SOUL**

BIOSONG

Copyright © 2017 by Lloyd Fell

All rights reserved. No part of this book may be reproduced, stored, or transmitted by any means – whether auditory, graphical, mechanical or electronic – without written permission of both publisher and author, except in the case of brief excerpts used in critical articles and reviews. Unauthorised reproduction of any part of the work is illegal and punishable by law.

First published by BIOSONG (www.biosong.org) in 2017

Cover design by Lloyd and Penelope Fell

Poems by Rumi and Blake are in the public domain.

National Library of Australia

Cataloguing in Publication Entry

| | |
|---|---|
| Creator: | Fell L. R., author |
| Title: / Lloyd Fell | Dancing With the Unknown – Feelings and everyday mind and soul |
| ISBN: | 9780994333216 (paperback) |
| Subjects: | Emotions |
| | Soul |
| | Mind and body |
| | Human behaviour |
| | Social psychology |

To all my teachers

**NOTE**

Nothing written in this book is to be regarded as medical advice.

The names and identities of people referred to as my personal friends have been altered to preserve their anonymity.

*Man was made for Joy and Woe*
*And when this we rightly know*
*Thro' the World we safely go*
*Joy and Woe are woven fine*
*A Clothing for the Soul divine*
*Under every grief and pine*
*Runs a joy with silken twine*

**William Blake – Auguries of Innocence (1803)**

*This being human is a guest house.*
*Every morning a new arrival.*

*A joy, a depression, a meanness,*
*some momentary awareness comes*
*as an unexpected visitor.*

*Welcome and entertain them all!*
*Even if they're a crowd of sorrows,*
*who violently sweep your house*
*empty of its furniture,*
*still, treat each guest honourably.*
*He may be clearing you out*
*for some new delight.*

*The dark thought, the shame, the malice,*
*meet them at the door laughing,*
*and invite them in.*

*Be grateful for whoever comes,*
*because each has been sent*
*as a guide from beyond.*

**Rumi - The Guest House (c. 1250)**

How are you feeling?
Me too.

Did he really want to know, you think
I think
I have a feeling . . . yes, I would like to know,
But
That's not easy because we deal in words.
Not quite the same.
But words can point to feelings, can't they?
Sometimes.

Every day it's the same, really
Is it?
Well, there are so many feelings; they come and go
That's all there is to it?
Enjoy the good ones, suffer the bad ones . . .
Attend to everything.
Of course.
Attend.

Let's chat some more?
If you like.

# Table of contents

Prelude .................................. 1
Chapter 1 ....... What Happened Today? ................. 3
Chapter 2 ....... Proper Use of the Mind? ............... 7
Chapter 3 ....... My Mind and I ....................... 15
Chapter 4 ....... The Function of the Mind ............. 21
Chapter 5 ....... The Importance of Stress ............. 29
Chapter 6 ....... What we Need is Love ................. 39
Chapter 7 ....... Recognising the Unknown .............. 43
Chapter 8 ....... Hidden Mind ......................... 49
Chapter 9 ....... Emotions, Feelings and Thoughts ........ 55
Chapter 10 ...... The Magic of Social Engagement ......... 67
Chapter 11 ...... Shared Meaning ....................... 75
Chapter 12 ...... Everyday Love ........................ 81
Chapter 13 ...... Attention and Awareness .............. 87
Chapter 14 ...... Too Much Self ........................ 95
Chapter 15 ...... Suffering ........................... 101
Chapter 16 ...... Courage to Change ................... 109
Chapter 17 ...... Values .............................. 117
Chapter 18 ...... A Need for Beauty ................... 125
Chapter 19 ...... Story, Song and Music ............... 131
Chapter 20 ...... The Feeling of Meaning .............. 137
Coda ................................... 143
Acknowledgments ....................... 145

# Prelude

A baby is born into the world, alive and well. What a wonder aliveness is and how precious! Mother clasps baby gently to her bosom and feels the pulse of life in the baby's heartbeat and her own. This is the fundamental connectedness we call love.

This is a book about love and why love is a biological necessity – an indispensable facilitator for the human mind. Without love we would not have flourished as a species and may not even have survived. There are more challenges ahead because man's inhumanity against his own kind, personal greed and disregard for his environment are serious threats to our existence and there is much human suffering. As we alienate ourselves from the natural world and our technology-driven lives take on more joyless urgency our mental health deteriorates because we are neglecting our most important attribute – naturally healthy minds practising love.

I almost lost my own mind – or the proper use of it, anyway – many years ago and I am grateful for the lessons learned in finding it again along with some glimpses of what I take to be my soul.

During my lifetime of researching animal physiology and behaviour I always yearned to connect the objective science with the subjective, first-person, experience that is one's reality. To do this we need to explain more about our feelings. Science and psychology have now accommodated emotions alongside rationality in explaining our mind but have not yet done justice to the feelings, which are the basic measure of our wellbeing. This is especially important because the neglect of our feeling function and the associated loss of meaning are common problems today.

In this book I am using my own life experience and past research on stress, together with what I have found to be the most useful ideas from science and psychology, to explain how I believe love works in one's life and in the world. As in my previous book, *Mind and Love – The Human Experience*, a biological framework that I attribute mainly to Humberto Maturana provides the foundation for my story.

## Chapter 1

## What Happened Today?

Life is an everyday occurrence – thankfully! When I awoke this morning I experienced the excitement I always feel if I can go straight to my office and resume my writing, there being no other commitments. I could describe my office and desk and my expectant walk down the hallway, but I cannot tell you exactly what this feels like inside. I wish I could, but my feelings are the most personal part of my experience and the hardest to share. The well-meant words 'I know what you're going through' can only ever be an approximation. I can give you some idea of what it feels like but that is a commentary on the feelings, not the feelings themselves. A substantial part of what I am feeling is still shrouded in the subconscious depths of my mind that I refer to in a general way as my emotions.

In writing this book I'm assuming that this *affect* (or emotional experience) is also our most immediate experience – the mind's leading edge. Something is happening in our subconscious minds a few moments before we become conscious of it. Thoughts follow quickly, of course, to grasp hold of the conscious experience. Over time these thoughts form themselves into a narrative that becomes our *story*. So I'm suggesting that our everyday experience occurs in two stages: we undergo it and then we evaluate it, to see what it *means* and to share it with others.

This ongoing narrative our mind creates is extremely important to us because it's a historical thread of meaning that holds everything that happens together in a way that makes sense. Our subconscious emotional experience also has a history, which influences the meaning we make. We need that sense of meaning – without it we are in big trouble! I think of it as a subjective feeling of satisfaction that, even with some holes in it for doubts and worry, tells us enough about where this experience came from and where it might be heading for us to *feel* okay. And it is how we feel that matters most!

My aim in this book is to turn the spotlight onto the feelings themselves; to bring the feelings into focus would be a better metaphor because they can be shy and elusive. They are not the same as emotions because the emotions are subconscious whereas the feelings are part of our conscious awareness. They are also not identical to our thoughts as I mentioned above; there is more to our feelings than is captured in the commentary made by our thinking. Feelings occupy some middle ground in the space between our *affect* and our *story*, both of which tend to claim them, so they may disappear back into the invisible depths of our emotions or become reconstituted as part of our story. My point in this book is that even the vaguest feeling we experience plays an important part in the business of our mind.

We can make our explanation of the mind as complicated or as simple as we like. I confess to being a brazen over-simplifier in this regard, but I do value and respect the science behind what I'm saying. I know it's presumptuous of me to try to say something useful and new about such a huge subject in a short book. I claim no great standing in the fields of neuroscience or psychology (though I published research papers about them) nor do I subscribe to the doctrine of any particular religion. I am drawing on my experience of life, my own research on stress (from my PhD onwards) and my continuing obsession for reading everything I can get my hands on about the mind, particularly the science.

Something else I hadn't planned also happened today. (Isn't it always the way!) I got a call to meet up with a friend of mine whom I'll call Alastair (though it's not his real name, of course). Alastair is going through a very bad time and his mind is filled with despair. He likes to talk at length about all the unfortunate things that have happened to him, mostly due to bad luck or caused by other people as he sees it. Whether his story is factual or not, it feels true for him. The meaning of his existence is captured in that story and it manifests in the way he feels and I can see he has been through tough times. He says his life is pointless and he can see no reason for going on. He is desperately lonely and avoids personal relationships except with a few of us who have also been through hard times ourselves. Speaking with him makes me wonder what would make the difference between his present state of mind and what we call wellness or wellbeing?

I think of wellbeing, or being well, as simply the sum of our good feelings and I think of feelings as the silent harbingers of meaning. The kind of meaning that sustains us as we strive to live well seems to me to include subtle properties that cannot entirely be captured in words. What I know is my story, which I will endeavour to tell you here, but the way I understand it depends also on my emotional history as that manifests in my feelings today. What I have to say includes quite a lot of biological science, but if I told you only that it may not engage with your feelings at all so there would not be much meaning of the kind that can be shared between us. Without shared meaning there isn't much fun in life. I try to connect meaningfully with Alastair and the only way I know to do this is to listen to him and respond with an attitude I have come to call *love*.

I think of this love, not as some kind of virtue, but as a natural product of my aliveness that we surely all have as part of our minds, which stems from the connectedness of the whole natural world. An Australian Aboriginal man, Big Bill Neidjie, wrote a book called *Story About Feeling* in which he identified himself as, amongst other things, a tree, a star and a goanna, which he said were 'all working with you . . . same as you . . . all the time.' The German biologist/philosopher, Andreas Weber, inspires me with his books about aliveness and the idea that feelings are the predispositions of all living things – the expression of mind throughout the natural world, holding it all together in a process he calls *The Biology of Wonder*.

What happened for each of us today is important because it is connected to what happened everywhere in the phenomenon of life of which one's own mind is a tiny part. My website is called *Biosong* because I think that life sings and we are all invited to sing along.[1] Music exemplifies and conveys the essence of aliveness – and the human mind – which is *movement*, not necessarily from place to place because most of it is internal. Without movement there would be no life. That baby would have been 'stillborn.'

---

[1] www.biosong.org

## Chapter 2

## Proper Use of the Mind?

What is it about one's mind that creates feelings of wellbeing or, on the other hand, feelings of despair? Here I am thinking about ordinary people in everyday situations and the subject is wellness. If I need to refer to diagnosed mental illness at times, I want you to know that I leave it entirely up to others to determine where the boundary is drawn between wellness and disease. The fact that I might not always agree with them is not the subject of this book.

I used to think about the minds of the animals (and even the plants) on the farm where I was growing up because they were part of my life every day. Mostly barefooted in those days, I enjoyed the feeling of treading on earth, grass and stones even though it was painful sometimes and I engaged with the minds of the farm animals as I learned from an early age how to handle them in different situations. Biology came naturally to me at school and from my very first lectures in animal physiology at university I craved to learn more about how the brain and body give us this experience of mind, which I thought was the bedrock of biology – the very core of our existence for every living thing.

Naively I wondered if there is an optimal or proper way of using one's mind that produces the best kind of experience and also *what happens if you lose the proper use of your mind?* My story begins with a personal answer to the second question. My own experience is that it happens so gradually you don't realise anything is wrong until there is a crisis of some sort. In my case it was a combination of marriage and financial problems, reduced output and missed opportunities at work and overwhelmingly bad feelings, mostly caused by an unhealthy habitual need to consume alcohol.[2]

One's story changes during the course of this downhill slide. My childhood farm experience was rather blissful but when I went away to university at 16 years of age I was painfully shy and socially inept so I was often anxious. Drinking alcohol made me feel better in social situations. Up to that point I believe I had a lively imagination that gave me some inner confidence because I felt there were natural resources inside me that enabled wellbeing. I read a lot and created my own adventure stories, which had fanciful characters, danger-filled plots and thoroughly happy endings and at my tiny primary school in the countryside I used to tell these stories in serial fashion to the other children. I now regard imagination as a precious part of my mind because my life got worse as it gradually dried up.

Over the next 20 years my own story narrowed noticeably as my feelings became gradually more dependent on things outside of myself. Neglecting my inner resources I used alcohol, relationships, sport and success at work to make me feel good so I needed progressively more of these as each year passed. In this dark period I struggled with abject and chronic dissatisfaction, severe anxiety that came and went and bouts of despair that became more frequent as time went on. My imagination gradually became a place of false refuge in which unhelpful fantasies were getting mixed up with my actual experience. My story lost touch with reality, though I didn't realise this was happening. I now think of this narrowing of meaning as a deterioration in the feeling function of my mind.

I also see it as an *improper* use of my mind but am grateful for it nonetheless because it enabled me to see more clearly, when I started to recover, what it is about my mind that works well and what doesn't work. I became aware of the number of other people who were suffering from a lack of mental wellness. Suicide rates are increasing steadily, especially among young people. The jails and hospitals are overflowing – mentally-disturbed young people flooding the jails and older people with failing

---

[2] I am not trying to define or use the terms *alcoholism*, *addiction* or *dependency* in this book, but will focus instead on *habits* and the role they play in our mind.

minds putting pressure on the hospital system. The incidence of reported anxiety and depression has escalated in many countries today with a staggering amount of personal suffering and loss of productivity. A popular American author, Scott Stossel, gives a sobering account in his book, *My Age of Anxiety*, of the extent of this problem and the lack of any obvious solution.

Attempts to deal with this fall into two categories. If it is due to the biological circumstances of individuals, both genetic and environmental in origin, then medical intervention is the most obvious answer and the resources available for treatment have multiplied rapidly. As more is learned about chemical imbalances in the brain and body, new pharmaceutical 'fixes' roll off the production line. Stossel explains how widespread is the use of mood-altering drugs, how common are their side-effects and how inconsistent have been their benefits. Yet it's also true that many a potential suicide or broken life (including his own) has been rescued by these drugs.

The second category of healing, favoured by opponents of 'Big Pharma' and critics of prescriptive psychiatry, is to harness one's own inner resources, which I'm calling the better use of the mind. Stossel tried this too and he states poignantly that he would dearly like to unlock the cabinet of truly effective inner resources but he finds himself 'fumbling with the keys.' This is the situation in the developed world today with both a widespread reliance on mood-altering substances and an equally widespread, intuitive desire to find and use more natural means of feeling good – or at least okay.

At the age of 37 I did not feel okay. I was swamped with self-pity and felt empty inside; there were two gaping holes in my existence. One was where my self-esteem should have been. Gradually I had lost confidence in myself as an individual to the point of actually hating myself at times. Driven by doubts about my autonomy and ability to survive I told lies and developed a bravado based on fantasies that were the best my now-limited imagination could come up with to get me out of this prison for brief periods. My story had become so bleak there seemed to be no way out into the sunlight again – in effect, no hope.

The other hole was that my relationships had mostly dried up. My first marriage was 'on the rocks' and most of my 'friends' were drinking buddies whom I didn't really like anyway. My loneliness carried with it the feeling that, because I was unlovable, I had never really been loved very much by anyone, which made me feel sorry for myself in a way that is poisonous for any kind of relationship. That was my story so I believed it. I imagined unrealistic ways of being connected to other people and lived in these fantasies instead of in reality. I felt I had become disconnected from the world. These were seriously bad feelings as anyone who has experienced them would know but with hindsight I can also see there were a few saving graces about the way my mind worked that I will mention later.

You don't have to live my particular story to experience these two holes in your life to some degree; we all have bad feelings about ourselves and our relationships at times. A Sydney psychiatrist, Julian Short, in a book called *An Intelligent Life*, identified (1) perceived deficiencies as an *individual* (not liking yourself) and (2) perceived difficulties with *relationships* (feeling lacking in love) as being the root of almost all the mental distress that he and other clinicians encounter in their patients.

I suggest that these are, in a nutshell, the consequences of losing the proper use of one's mind. I experienced them to such a degree that it took me years to recover completely after I stopped drinking alcohol at the age of 37; you may have handled them better. The good news, in my view, is that those symptoms tell us what we need to know about our mind and soul to make better use of them.

In short they tell us that the function of our mind is to *maintain and promote (1) our healthy autonomy as individuals and (2) our connections with the world through loving relationships*. This simple way of describing it didn't mean a great deal to me at first but today it feels like the most important thing I have ever learned about the mind.

My love affair with the science of physiology in particular and biology in general eventually led me to see more clearly how this works in my everyday experience. I will be explaining how the paradigm-changing research on the biology of cognition that emanated from Humberto

Maturana and Francisco Varela gave me a new framework for understanding the human mind and my own situation. Subsequently I drew from the work of many other medical scientists, three in particular who are featured in this book. They are Stephen Porges, Jaak Panksepp and Iain McGilchrist.

The science is not the whole story. The objectivity of scientific thinking provides us with mechanistic explanations so we know how things work. But I'm not talking here about my car or my computer; I'm talking about my life! The pain and anguish I experienced during those dark times woke me up to the possibility that I might never overcome my lack of wellness if I continued to use my mind as I had been doing; in fact the harder I tried to think my way into a better way of living the more hopeless my situation seemed to be.

That dawning realisation of my powerlessness was the starting point. I reached a stage where I wanted to change so badly I was ready to give up some *self*-reliance and admit that there might be more to this problem than I could ever figure out using only my rational mind. I had unwittingly developed an inflated sense of what I knew and what I didn't know. Even the idea that I could control the proper use of my mind was a form of scientific hubris. Of course I was aware that there were things I didn't know and might never know but I didn't believe they were important and I saw no need to heed or respect what was unknown for its own sake. My pain triggered *ego-deflation* and my mind entertained a new kind of humility that was not primarily to do with other people – it meant deferring to the fact that what was completely unknown to me was apparently very influential in my life. I gradually came to believe it could be the largest influence of all.

The commonest way of explaining this is to imagine it as an external supernatural force that we call God, but I've never entirely given up the alternate idea that it might be just a property of all human beings that we can't explain. Either way it's a mystery. It seems to relate to my respect for the natural world – the wonder of life itself, which was instilled in my mind growing up on the farm. I think of it now as a decidedly better way of using my mind, anyway, that stems from the fact pointed out by Sam

Harris in his book, *Waking Up: A Guide to Spirituality without Religion*, that 'there is more to understanding the human condition than science and secular culture generally admit.' Later I came to agree with the view expressed by the eminent astronomer, Carl Sagan, in his *Varieties of Scientific Experience*, that 'if we ever reach a point where we think we thoroughly understand who we are and where we came from, we will have failed.'

This shift in my mind and soul did not diminish my enthusiasm for science; in fact I felt that I could now utilise what we learn from science more effectively. In Chapter 7 I will return to this idea of recognising *the unknown*. It might sound like a limitation to the use of the mind but I see it now as a strength, even though it implies that there is some kind of 'larger-than-self' responsibility or authority directly involved in human experience.

I talk with Alastair about this and he thinks I am mistaken. He believes there can be no higher power than the ability of the human mind to reason logically and this will be sufficient to work out what is going wrong and show us how to solve all our problems. He says that both God on high and mysterious forces within us are created by our imagination and we should only trust objectively-known facts. I do agree about the imagination but somehow I suspect it is actually the most important part of one's mind. In feeling love for him I try to respect his point of view and I can do that most of the time. He is a beautiful man who cares deeply for others and for himself and even though his life feels so grim at this time I have a strong sense of hope that he will also find the kind of satisfaction and pleasure that I enjoy today. I think there is an ambivalent quality to our mind whereby we can't really appreciate satisfaction unless we have known frustration as well.

Regarding the power of the unknown he may be right but I am concerned, first and foremost, with my own experience. The point about experience that is fundamental to my story is that it is ultimately all we have to rely on to know about our mind. We explain everything in terms of our own experience – even the lecturers who attribute what they say to another source are doing this. We come to believe in a certain way of explaining ourselves and our world if our experience rewards us with some satisfaction and a state of mind that we call happiness. This book is about what works for me.

## Chapter 3

## My Mind and I

The relationship with one's mind is a curious business. I can't avoid talking about my mind as if it is something separate from me, yet I also think of it as being me – the most obvious manifestation of me. I can't escape from it into a separate body; that wouldn't work anyway because my mind is there as well. It's been known for thousands of years (in yoga, for example) that body movements and postures affect one's mental state. Plenty of research shows that physical exercise influences the mind and can be a powerful healing force.

To believe that I am what I think I am has quite a good philosophical pedigree but the assumption that I therefore know my mind and can control it is misleading. Some people claim to have great power over their minds but for most of us it's all too obvious that our mind is either a disobedient servant or even our master. Try telling yourself to go to sleep or stop thinking about your very sick friend or your new 'toy.' Saying to someone, or to yourself, that you should not be anxious or depressed is as futile as trying to stop the tide coming in.

Of course we all know that a large part of our mind is unconscious or *subconscious*. It can generally be trusted to run all the things we take for granted such as our breathing, our digestion, our heartbeat and so on. It also seems to influence our thoughts and our behaviour in subtle ways that we try to decipher in psychology but which still remain shrouded in mystery. My experience of ego-deflation did not diminish my desire to know more about psychology either but it gave me an ever-growing respect for this mystery. The term I use for respecting the unknown is *spirituality*. I now believe that this is what was missing during the dark period of my life.

A well-known spiritual teacher, Eckhart Tolle, began his first book, *The Power of Now*, with a description of his own life-changing experience regarding his mind. Until age 29 he lived with 'almost continuous anxiety interspersed with periods of suicidal depression.' His recurring thought: 'I cannot live with myself' brought an awareness one day that there seemed to be two of him: an 'I' and a 'self' that the 'I' couldn't live with – and one of these could be an imposter. This set in motion his life of spiritual teaching based on recognising the aspects of one's thinking that claim to be real but are actually false. I came to believe that these lies the mind tells were obstacles that prevented me from discovering the proper use of my mind. When people said to Tolle: 'I want what you have' he would say: 'you have it already. You just can't feel it because your mind is making too much noise.'

My experience has been to try to understand my mind's noisy self-deception. Its lies include the idea that I am not loved, that other people are somehow fundamentally better (or in some cases, worse) than I am, and that I have certain weaknesses and habits that are so entrenched they could never be changed. These thoughts are a certain kind of **self-consciousness**, which is a very narrow, self-centred perspective given that I am actually just one member of an entire human race and a whole ecosystem of other beings. We are one amongst many, totally dependent on other living things for our survival.

The imposter in Tolle's explanation is the very notion of the egoic *self*. An inflated ego creates an illusory self that makes judgments and thinks it knows things and can control things that are way beyond its reach. I have found that the harder I try to protect and support a self-centred version of 'myself' the more prone I am to self-deception. Getting to 'know yourself' often seems to include justifying your bad habits on the grounds that they are simply who you are. Whenever one's mind is not engaged in a task or interacting with other people it is naturally drawn towards self-reflection. Neuroscience has confirmed this and demonstrated that the *default* region of one's brain becomes more active when the mind is 'doing nothing.' The imagination is like a simulator running different scenarios, which can, as in my case, become narrower and bleaker if self-centredness takes over and we lose touch with our world.

Our saving grace is the fact that we do not exist in isolation. Every human being is an ecosystem that includes millions of other microorganisms living inside us and on our skin; we inhabit a biosphere of plants and other animals that is life-sustaining only through the symbiotic interaction of one with the other. And no matter how lonely we become there are always other humans around somewhere. It's true that I need to have my autonomy to be self-governing as an individual but if I see this in context I realise that there could be no autonomy without connectedness to others – no me without my relationships.

Perhaps you have been walking in the wilderness or standing on a mountaintop at sunrise or looking out across the ocean as the sun goes down and felt a sense of awe that you are such a small part of something much bigger than yourself. A smaller sense of self seems to enable a larger sense of belonging. So artificial is our modern living environment that it's easy to forget we are a part of Nature. Alienation from our natural world has the effect of narrowing our consciousness so that our sense of self becomes an ego-inflation, which leads to the kind of problems I was having that I know affect others as well.

It was through relationships with others that my life was turned around. The important new field of **social neuroscience** has grown from the idea that our individual minds are actually co-created with others through our relationships. We are not just individuals who get into relationships; we become the individuals we are because of what we do in our relationships. So there is no such thing as a single brain operating in isolation; the brain is a social organ that is shaped by our experience in the world.

I think this is an important clue regarding the proper use of our mind because it shifts our attention from self toward relationships. In this book I will be speaking about three different kinds of relationship – three different levels at which this all-important connectedness can occupy our minds. The first and most obvious is with the world around us, especially other people; the second is with ourselves, which implies humility; the third one is our relationship with what is unknown. The way we do this is by directing our attention, which is a significant part of what our mind does as we shall see. When self-centredness fills too much of the space in our minds there is insufficient room for the relationships with others or with the unknown.

There is solid science to explain how connectedness works, but once again the science is not the whole story because it does not explain one's relationship with the unknown. Again, I have to rely on my actual experience to inform and validate that part of my mind. So my explanation of mind throughout this book will be part science and part personal experience. I am satisfied with that, though I have to say my friend Alastair is not.

He believes, like all my most ardent scientific colleagues, that we need to explain everything in terms of cause and effect before we should believe it and that it's only a matter of time before this will be achieved by science. My position is that for now – and the foreseeable future – that is not the case. I am reminded of the supposedly prophetic statement made by Lord Kelvin, the British Chief Scientist at the end of the 19$^{th}$ century, that there is nothing more to discover in physics now that the nature of the electromagnetic field has been unravelled. Within a few decades the revolutionary theories of relativity and quantum mechanics had come into being!

I find the mechanistic explanations of science very helpful for understanding my mind. But they are incomplete because my everyday experience extends beyond the reaches of that science. My feelings include subtle qualities such as wonder, beauty, hope, a joyful surprise and a sense of belonging or of loneliness that give a meaning to my life that I feel I could not do without.

Einstein is often quoted as saying that 'imagination is more important than knowledge' because knowledge is limited to what we know now whereas imagination can extend far wider across all possibilities. He is also supposed to have said that 'if you want your children to be intelligent, read them fairy tales.' It's a significant biological fact that our brain chemistry responds just the same to what we imagine we are doing as it does when we are actually doing it. I have no difficulty including the unknown in my imagination because it has proved to be a successful way to use my mind. My mind and I are on better terms today than they were years ago.

Of course many famous scientists respect the unknown so I am in good company. My first physiology professor gave me a copy of *Man the Unknown* by Nobel laureate, Alexis Carrel, who was a famous physiologist who thought the material realm of the body was incomplete without the soul. Also as a student I devoured books like *Animal Nature and Human Nature* by W. H. Thorpe, one of the founders of the science of ethology, who concluded that our human consciousness was a unique form of meaning that he called 'religious.' The philosopher, Alfred North Whitehead, was a great champion of the human mind yet he also criticised our 'absurd trust' in the 'adequacy of our knowledge' that has seduced science into claiming to be the final word on everything.

The aspect of mind science that has expanded most rapidly in recent decades is known as **embodied cognition**. It is a recognition of the fact that the process of one's mind includes our muscles, heart, lungs, gut and every other organ and part of the body as well as the brain. There are internal patterns of connectedness throughout our body, both neural and hormonal, that manifest in our behaviour, thoughts and feelings. They affect everything our mind does. *Intelligence in the Flesh* is the phrase used by Guy Claxton in his book, which is subtitled: *Why Your Mind Needs Your Body Much More Than It Thinks*. For convenience in this book I refer to the internal patterns of connectedness as our emotions.

Claxton argues that intelligence does not consist of controlling your emotions with reason, nor is it a different kind of meaning that exists separately in your emotions; it is an amalgamation of the entire brain/body process that we experience as meaning in our feelings. He writes: 'Feelings are somatic events that embody our values and concerns. They signal what we care about: what gives our lives meaning and direction. Our hopes and fears arise from the resonance of our organs in response to events.' He suggests that without feelings and intuition our intelligence would lose touch with the subtlety and complexity of our everyday experience. If that happened our mind would fail in its primary function of giving us our identity and connecting us to our surroundings.

Much of the scientific explanation of embodied cognition still implies a separation of mind and body. If we are to understand aliveness we need to move beyond this Cartesian split and embrace the wholeness of the mind in our everyday experience. Our being is also our doing. We need the visceral to grasp the cerebral. Aliveness is an experience; we also call it animation, which means movement. The distinction between animate and inanimate helps us to think of mind and body as one.

## Chapter 4

## The Function of the Mind

I want to describe the mind in terms of what it does rather than what it is, because of course it is not a substance, it is a *process* that we are immersed in at all times even as we are trying to explain how it works. In the English language we love naming *things* but we can be quite vague about *processes*. More than 50% of our words are nouns and another 25% are adjectives that embellish the nouns whereas verbs, the doing words, make up less than 15% of our language. We are most comfortable with solid substance and rather wary of ever-changing flux, even though Heraclitus alerted us long ago to the reality that 'no man ever steps in the same river twice for it's not the same river and he's not the same man.' There is no such thing as an unchanging mind – no object to point to that will still be there a moment later. We need to imagine it as a moving force.

I think it's probably impossible to work out the function of the mind by simply observing human behaviour and trying to interpret it. Psychology gradually became more scientific whereby minds are manipulated experimentally to develop mechanistic, cause-and-effect explanations but these still don't get to the bottom of things. The alternative to that top-down approach for studying the mind is the bottom-up approach of basic biology. It is by studying the simplest living things and working our way through the evolutionary tree to humans that we can understand most clearly how the mind works.

The man who convinced me about this approach was the Chilean biologist, Humberto Maturana, whom I got to know personally from his visits to Australia and through correspondence. He is a legendary figure in international biology yet I think his contribution to mind science is still vastly underrated. For one thing it was his paradigm-changing 'biology of cognition' that explained the word *'love'* in a scientific way for the first time. Together with a former student and equally famous pioneer of mind science, Francisco Varela, he showed how the most basic biology could open windows for us to see things differently about the human mind. Varela's untimely death in 2001 at the age of 54 was a great loss.

Maturana was born in 1928 in Santiago, Chile, where he first studied medicine, then transferred to biology and went to London to work with J. Z. Young, a famous pioneer of mind biology. During PhD studies at Harvard Maturana co-authored a notable paper called *What the Frog's Eye Tells the Frog's Brain* after which he returned to Santiago where he remained rather separate from the mainstream of mind science, although he attended international meetings and his papers were widely discussed. I enjoyed talking with him about the freedom he felt in being somewhat isolated and developing his highly original ideas with his students. He subsequently founded, with Ximena Dávela, a unique centre for cultural biology called *Matriztica*.

I said that mind is the bedrock of biology because without that concept it's hard to imagine living things existing. From the very beginning they had to distinguish themselves from their immediate surroundings in order to be living things. The simple cell wall of the original single-celled being (possibly a bacterium) was the first example of a dividing line between the inside and the outside of an organism. This provided a mechanism for living things to become viable units in their own right by maintaining their internal processes in the face of an outside world that followed different rules, constantly changing independently of them and not necessarily in their best interests. When the ability to reproduce was added so that new generations were possible it was the beginning of a very long line of entities that we call living things because they can coexist with their surroundings in ecological niches while preserving an individual identity by having a 'mind of their own.'

So in biological terms mind and life are one and the same. It requires an imaginative leap to think this way because our common usage of the word 'mind' gives it peculiarly human characteristics and it has been closely associated with the workings of our brain for obvious reasons. When someone is on a life-support machine because his brain seems to be ruined he is said to be a 'vegetable' and to have no mind but strictly speaking his most basic life and mind still exist until the connecting tubes are removed. The human brain is an incredible organ but it is not our mind and its processes are not the full extent of our mind process. What scientists (particularly neuroscientists) tend to do is to explain everything in terms of the bit that they know something about. They take the whole of reality and experience to be the same as the part that their methodology has revealed to them without considering the broader context within which that part operates. The explanation sounds good and it can be useful though it can also be misleading and it contributes to the hubris of thinking we know more than we do.

One reason we think our mind is uniquely human is that we have tried to distinguish ourselves from the natural world and assumed that, because it is different, we can own it and control it, forgetting that we are simply part of it; we are alive because the biosphere supports us. As Andreas Weber and others have suggested we can think of mind as a universal predisposition to respond and adapt that all living things have in common so we are not an isolated case – we are simply part of the ecology.

If you look through a microscope at a primitive being like an amoeba, which has no brain or nervous system, 'swimming' in its liquid world, you will notice that it can move away from a toxic substance or move towards a source of food. If you think about it you will recognise this as the most elementary example of a mind at work; it is the most rudimentary 'decision-making' experience. The simplest animal – or plant – 'knows' what to do to try to stay alive. Every living organism has an ability to connect with its surroundings *meaningfully* – that is, in a way that meets the needs of its autonomous existence. Some form of movement is a characteristic of all life. The amoeba's ability to move is very limited and living things that move about are generally animals, which have a brain. For plants the movement is mainly internal although they are able to grow towards moisture and light and produce spectacular flowers and fruit.

The way living things adapt themselves to particular environments shows their mind also to be the basic instrument for learning. They are trying to conserve that adaptation through generations and when large populations achieve this that species will thrive, at least for a time. Evolution is the name for this ongoing process of adaptation, but it is misleading to think of it as a competitive 'survival of the fittest' as Darwinian thinking is often portrayed. Biology went through a stage of worshipping 'selfish genes' as the primary instruments of evolution. It turned out that the role of individual genes had been exaggerated and it is now recognised to be a much more 'epigenetic' and cultural process.

Consider the most basic things that you and I have to achieve every day. To stay alive we must maintain our internal environment within quite narrow limits even though our external environment may get too cold or too hot or threaten us in any number of ways. We could not do this without a subconscious process known as homeostasis, but we need to make lots of conscious decisions, too, to obtain the shelter, clothing and nutrients that we need. We have to notice what is happening around us and decide where and how we will situate ourselves in our world, not just for survival, right down to the company we keep and the feelings that we share with others.

There are two quite different kinds of process involved. Internally it is stability and continuity that we need – a coherent ongoing process that will essentially look after itself as long as we provide it with fuel. This came to be called biological **autonomy**. The outside world is foreign and not part of this internal process except that we need to engage with it, firstly to know what threats or opportunities exist and secondly to obtain our fuel. We need oxygen, water and food as well as social companions. To do this we must make appropriate **connections**, reaching out strategically with our senses and opening our protective barrier just enough to take in whatever we need. The task of connecting optimally at all times is a tricky one indeed!

If you hark back to what happens when we lose the proper use of our mind I hope that might become more meaningful in the light of this basic biology. I was losing my sense of identity on the one hand and my relationships on the other. A living system cannot exist without being both *autonomous* **and** *connected* to its world. Those are the essential requirements for life and our wellbeing depends on how efficiently both of these functions are achieved. We live with a myriad of subtle threats to our autonomy and obstacles to our relationships, which is where our wellbeing suffers. The solution to our problems lies in optimising both our strength as individuals and the strength of our relationships, which is a challenge; it is never going to be easy because these two could be pulling in opposite directions. In Chapter 6 I will speak about love as the phenomenon that integrates these two forces.

Autonomy means self-governing, which begins with being self-producing (or *autopoietic*, to use Maturana's term). Instead of being created by the action of outside forces such as a motor car is put together in a factory, a living thing is re-created in each moment from itself, as long as it has a functional mind and an adequate connection. We go on creating a new version of ourselves moment by moment until we can no longer do this, whereupon we die. Self-government does not mean separateness; in fact its connectivity is crucial, hence the importance of paying attention to our relationships. This gives us another working definition of what mind is like: it's *the process that keeps us connected to the world in such a way that we retain our individual identities – our autonomy*.

The barrier that separates us from the outside world sufficiently well for our internal process to be autonomous does not block out all outside influences, of course. The fluctuations in the outside world will have some impact on our insides, triggering adjustments, slowing down or speeding up some processes, producing reactions of various kinds. In the next Chapter we will see that this is what we commonly refer to as **stress**. As we adapt better to our circumstances the perturbations become less severe. As long as these outside forces don't overwhelm and destroy our autonomous existence we will survive.

The crucial point is that *we are not determined by our surroundings* even though we are affected by them. This way of thinking not only came into my life after I emerged from the dark times, it has found its proper place in the culture of biological science only during my lifetime as well.

When I started out in research the way we talked and thought about physiology (and psychology) was built around the principle of *stimulus and response*. The outside world created the stimuli and the organism responded, sometimes in a thoroughly predictable way (like a kneejerk reflex), but usually with individual variability. Behind this way of thinking is the simplistic, but pervasive, idea that the stimuli were the cause and what happened in our lives was the effect, albeit modulated by our internal state. I think this largely subconscious mindset has lured us towards our dependence on external remedies for any internal malaise. Certainly my own dark times were a manifestation of this.

Nevertheless, we can be thankful that medical science thrived on that cause-and-effect way of thinking because, except for homeopathy, it is essentially allopathic, which means it treats disease by manipulating our system from the outside. We shouldn't forget that any external treatment is greatly assisted – often totally enabled – by the internal process of natural healing. The well-known placebo effect and the rather haphazard history of potions and remedies shows that this natural healing process usually does not get the credit it deserves. While there have been huge improvements in human health generally, this is not the case for mental health, which has probably deteriorated. Some chronic diseases such as fibromyalgia and other auto-immune conditions that are said to be stress-related are also more prevalent today.

Mind (like life) is an extraordinary kind of force because it enables us to **be and belong** at the same time. It also seems to defy the physical law of entropy whereby matter must run down to a more disordered state inevitably. Living things differ from physical systems in that they actually become more complex and more ordered as they grow and develop – although they eventually die and decay. They achieve this by drawing energy from their physical surroundings as long as the life-force continues. Though we might understand the function of mind in a practical way we can only wonder about what mystery is behind it, where it came from and where it will eventually take us.

My explanation of mind can be compared with that used by others, at least with those who have moved on from the simplistic notion that the mind is 'what the brain does' to the idea that the mind is a process that uses the brain and the body to do what it needs to do. Dan Siegel's latest book, *Mind: A Journey to the Heart of Being Human*, gives what is a widely used definition – that the mind is 'an embodied, relational process that regulates the flow of energy and information within and between us.' I like this because it shows the mind existing both *within* and *between* us but the problem is we still have to define and explain 'energy' and 'information,' which is actually not easy to do – it introduces other complications. This is a universal problem because we always explain something in terms of something else – as I have done by saying that the mind maintains autonomy through connectedness – but my hope is that we can imagine these biological phenomena a little more easily than 'energy' and 'information' because they are simply our feelings of *being and belonging*.

In the reality of our experience we think of our mind as a clever tool that enabled us to get through school, get a job, find a partner and enjoy knowing about all the things that make one's life interesting, enjoying play, appreciating beauty and feeling love. We may also think of it as a tormentor, the part that worries and frets, craving for certainty without ever finding it. It could also be the way your imagination connects you in wonder with something greater than yourself bringing feelings of awe and gratitude. Beneath all this stupendous range and richness of human experience is the mind's most basic function of enabling us to *be and belong*. That is the simplest way of describing it.

It is by keeping it simple that we get our priorities right for the use of our mind. When we forget those basics we introduce complications – as I know only too well from my own experience. This is when the lies that Tolle speaks about come into play. The complications lead to misconceptions about what we are supposed to be doing with our mind that manifest most often as *unnecessary judgments* and *inappropriate attempts to control*.

The personal opinions that arise in our thoughts are not the problem; they fuel the everyday conversation that we need to manage our affairs and bring about change. And meanings are themselves a kind of judgment that our mind is making. The problem is that *we tend to express far more detailed and more frequent judgments about other people and what is right and wrong than are actually necessary and we overdo the use of our mind to control and manipulate our circumstances and other people*.

In the Chapters ahead I will expand on the way that the labels we apply are limiting and the attempts to control are constraining the proper use of one's mind.

## Chapter 5

# The Importance of Stress

Rachael is another friend who had problems similar to mine and made a good recovery and nowadays I admire the way she handles any kind of stress in her life. She has a large family, runs a business and her life can be hectic but she likes to deal with things on the spot without allowing them to carry over. She was never a loner like I was – in fact she had a string of short-term relationships early on; she now has an affectionate, caring husband and several close friends with whom she can share the burden of any stress she encounters so she feels loved in her body and mind. Her life is not always great because she makes judgments and tries to control like I do, but she manages to avoid an accumulation of stress.

I probably notice this because I spent a large part of my life conducting research into the causes and consequences of stress, mainly in farm animals. This learning coincided with the worst of my dark times and all of my recovery so it was a combination of theory and practice that helped me to understand my own mind. My positive curiosity and lack of fear regarding stress was also one of the saving graces for my mind that I mentioned earlier, probably originating back on the farm where coping with stress seemed to be more matter of fact and commonplace. Meeting Maturana and learning about the work of Stephen Porges and Jaak Panksepp changed the way I understood stress and helped me to realise its importance.

The experience of stress is a normal and necessary part of our mind and life – our external circumstances perturb our internal state so that adjustments are required. Our mind supports both our autonomy and our connectedness, but these equally important needs are complementary, not alternatives, and they cannot both be totally satisfied. There has to be a certain amount of difference and tension because you would cease to exist as an individual if your mind and body were perfectly equilibrated with your surroundings. That nice sense of individuality and the subtle challenges of connecting well that make life interesting are also its basic requirements. There is always some stress, though we tend to notice it only when it becomes severe.

If stress is unpleasant we will try to avoid it. However, if we are to understand mind we must come to terms with the fact that aliveness is an engagement with the world and to turn away from all stress would be to turn away from life itself. We can avoid external physical forces but what is happening internally can't be ignored without harmful consequences. For stress that is purely physical the equation is simple: the greater the load we are under the more work our body is required to do. Our mind does its best to manage that. Similarly with stress from heat or cold or deprivation of water or food we must try to correct the imbalance between our internal state and the external circumstances or our lives are at risk. But most of our everyday experience of stress is more subtle than that and it is the core business of our mind.

Most everyday stress occurs in the form of psychological and behavioural adjustments that we need to make to *be and belong*. Our mind is designed to deal with the threats to our autonomy and the obstacles affecting our relationships in such a way that we feel okay; our efficacious responses to stress ensure our wellbeing. I'm suggesting in this book that we need love in our lives to do this well. My point here is that our mind is designed to use stress to our advantage rather than to suffer from it. We have in common with all mammals basic responses that Panksepp calls our instinctual or *primary emotions* that equip our brains and bodies to meet challenges in a positive way as they arise.

Many of us don't have Rachael's skill at dealing with situations on the spot nor her secure social relationships. Humans suffer more from stress than animals do because the demands on our mind are more complex and we tend to worry about it too much. Instead of the stimulus of nervous excitement we may feel the clammy hand of fear when we begin to doubt that we can adapt to the external pressure. Some people who play sport, for example, play better when they are under the most pressure while others play their worst at that time.

In surveys, people who say they have very meaningful lives also say there is more stress in their lives than others might have and they see a link between the two. They get their sense of meaning in part from meeting challenges successfully, which requires extra effort and skill, but brings satisfaction. Other research shows that adverse outcomes from stress depended more on people's attitudes to it than it did upon the level of stress. Regarding it as a challenge instead of a threat and making good use of the short-term resources it offers led to better outcomes. There is an important caveat here because simply trying harder with self-will may not be the best option as, for example, when my stubborn self-reliance was preventing me from getting well. To know when to push on with something and when to back off is never going to be easy.

Short-term stress that becomes part of the flow of your life does not have long-term adverse consequences but stress that is prolonged or recurring can seriously damage your health. It is most often the accumulation of short-term stresses that have not been dealt with that will become a prolonged (*i.e.* chronic) kind of stress and this is where stress does its damage. Our mind is such that to avoid or deny even minor stress will generally be worse than engaging with it. We need to be *more* conscientious about our connectedness when we are under pressure because that is how the mind relieves its tension and moves forward. We often do the reverse by isolating ourselves and trying to dismiss the problem. The way that Rachael utilises her loving relationships to help her put the stress into perspective and is not frightened to connect with it decisively and promptly is the way our mind is designed to live with stress.

I likened this process to singing and dancing together in a musical play I wrote in 1989 called *Stress: The Musical*. It was part of my own learning about stress to write and perform songs about the way the mind works because it seemed to help with the feeling of flow in my own mind.[3]

If we are injured or sick, like all animals, we tend to withdraw rather than reach out. This brings me to a very important qualification of what I have said about the beneficial nature of stress generally. Each experience of

---

[3] See www.biosong.org.

stress leaves some impression or imprint in the history of our mind, both subconscious and conscious. These are a natural part of our learning and adapting process and are mostly beneficial changes in brain and body connectivity. But if the stress is severe and inescapable, as it may be in children for example, that imprint becomes a wound that won't heal – or it heals like a scar – which is what we call *trauma*. There is structural damage to the brain that has been shown to disturb perception, numb one's sense of self, close down the imagination and in severe cases destroy the sense of time so that a past traumatic incident keeps intruding on the present experience.

Bessel van der Kolk's book, *The Body Keeps the Score*, is an insightful account of how the treatment of trauma has evolved in recent decades and why post-traumatic stress, which is an abnormal stress response, is much more widely recognised today. He calls it the 'hidden epidemic.' Front-line combat in a war zone (or in civilian shooting incidents nowadays) has always been recognised as traumatic though it is only in very recent wars that the large number of soldiers affected has been acknowledged. In textbooks as recently as 1980 the sexual abuse of children was said to be a rare occurrence and not a significant medical issue. It is now known that many millions of people have been traumatised in this way. The way the brain responds to everyday stress has been altered in these cases and the healing process can be slow and difficult and may not ever be complete.

The brain is not our mind, as I've said, but it is the main tool that our mind employs to operate successfully. It is the pattern of connectivity rather than the individual brain regions that best describes brain function. Just as our life experience is a constantly changing pattern of connectedness, so the internal connectivity of the brain and the body is the constantly changing pattern of our subconscious mind. The internal patterns of connection and our connectivity with the external world lead and follow one another in the dance of life.

The **brain stem** at the bottom end is sometimes called the 'reptilian' brain because it is the oldest part in evolutionary terms. Built onto that are the most important emotion-generating regions that are often sub-grouped as the **limbic system**, which all mammals have as well as us. What makes our brain so much larger than other animals is the part called the **cortex** that is folded and wraps over and around the rest. The pre-frontal cortex behind our forehead is where our unique thinking processes are generated. It is all incredibly interconnected and many areas that are crucial for our attention process, decision-making, awareness of danger and the experience of pleasure are deep within the cortex. I have already mentioned the *default zone* for self-reflection which extends from the medial frontal cortex into the limbic structures including the amygdala, hippocampus and hypothalamus.

Dealing with stress involves all of the brain beginning with the brain stem, which is the hub of our Autonomic Nervous System (ANS). This is the subconscious part of our nervous system that involves all our organs in the work of our mind in a process called self-regulation. It also contributes, through the cranial nerves, to our involuntary facial expression, our sight and hearing and our voice, which are critical parts of our social engagement. This is where the internal patterns of connection show up in the external patterns of behaviour and vice versa.

Two main processes, though they are only part of the story, have come to define stress in the textbook. The first, known as the HPA axis, is a cascade of hormones beginning in the brain (hypothalamus) through the pituitary gland to the outer part of the adrenal gland where cortisol and other steroids are released into the bloodstream. My research revolved around measurements of cortisol, which is still the most commonly used indicator of stress. Cortisol is needed, along with DHEA (dihydroepiandrosterone) and other growth factors to mobilise energy and strengthen everything our mind and body does. Also released are endorphins (the natural opiates) that reduce pain and produce feelings of wellbeing and oxytocin that eases anxiety and promotes trust and strong social bonds. These are all necessary resources for our mind and body.

It was this adrenal response following severe stress that Hans Selye had inflicted on laboratory rats that he used to coin the new term 'stress' in 1936. He called it the 'general adaptation syndrome' in its basic form though he focussed on its deleterious effects on health when it was prolonged. He distinguished between 'distress' and the helpful initial response to stress. The long-term over-production of cortisol weakens our immune system, which is the reason that prolonged stress makes us more susceptible to colds and flu, for example, and it is also said to predispose to depression and anxiety. It's worth noting that Selye's treatment of his rats was far more severe than anything we encounter in our everyday stress.

The second definitive aspect of the stress response is much more rapid and involves the brain stem and the ANS. The ability to keep everything in balance within our body – self-regulation – is managed by the ANS, which has two parts to it: one to speed things up and the other to slow things down. The arousing arm includes the hormone, adrenalin, which boosts heartrate and blood pressure to prepare you for action. This is called the fight-or-flight response to stress. The soothing arm of the ANS is unusual in that its main nerve, the vagus, does not run through the spinal column – it wanders down through your abdomen to reach the heart, lungs, digestive tract and every other organ. That warm feeling across your chest or comfortable feeling in your tummy when you are relaxed is almost certainly due to your vagus nerve.

It was Stephen Porges' 'polyvagal theory' that showed us why our human capacity for loving relationships is vital for our self-regulation and is our best antidote for stress. This is a crucial difference between humans and other animals. Porges is an American neurophysiologist whose work is summarised in his book *The Polyvagal Theory – Neurophysiological Foundations of Emotions, Attachment, Communication and Self-Regulation*. He too came to understand this biology by studying our evolution, in this case of the ANS.

Much earlier in evolution, cold-blooded animals like lizards had a rudimentary ANS as their survival system. It could pep them up or shut them down and they coped with stress mainly by shutting their metabolism down altogether as in hibernation during winter or the 'freeze' response (death-feigning) that helped to protect them against predators. We still have those immobilising nerve fibres as part of our 'dorsal vagus system' running from the *back* of our brain stem to our organs including our heart.

By the time mammals had evolved, such a drastic shutdown was highly inappropriate because the larger brain must have a constant supply of oxygen; in fact animals and newborn babies can die this way from sudden shock. Therefore the arousing part of the ANS had been beefed up to produce the fight-or-flight response. These nerve fibres connect to the brain through the spinal column and they stimulate heartrate, blood pressure and respiration to deal with the emergency. Thus the primary response to stress had evolved from a basic immobilisation to a form of mobilisation.

The mammals also introduced the suckling of their young that was an enormous impetus for what Stephen Porges calls our 'social engagement system' about which I will be saying much more. Our need to hold one another in our arms and our ability to do this is the foundation for our loving social relationships. It was the evolution of a new branch of the vagus nerve that made this possible. We have additional vagus nerve fibres running from the *front* of the brain stem to our organs that I refer to as the **new soothing ANS** and we have these because we needed more options than simply speeding up or shutting down to cope with the kinds of stress that we face all the time.

This new soothing ANS (or 'ventral vagus system') gave to humans an entirely new level of intimacy for social engagement because it enables *immobilisation without fear*. This kind of trust became absolutely crucial in recent human evolution because the only way we could survive against external threats was by banding together in close-knit communities. Nursing of the newborn was the precursor and the mother-infant relationship is the evolutionary basis for what we call relationships of love. The hormone, oxytocin, that enables milk letdown for suckling works closely with the new soothing ANS to promote trust and inter-personal bonding. Porges referred to love very aptly as 'an emergent property of the mammalian ANS.'

So we humans now have three different levels of stress response available to us. Our best strategy for handling stress is through the loving social engagement that is enabled by the new soothing ANS. The connecting of our minds and bodies with other humans keeps our adaptation flowing. Any experience that feels stressful can be better handled if you can talk to someone about it – not seeking judgments or opinions, just for the flowing connection. Holding someone's hand or feeling their touch on your arm have been shown to soothe the stress response and lessen pain. Porges showed that facial and vocal expression, body movement and interactive play are some of the best treatment modalities for post-traumatic stress. They exercise our unique social engagement system that is especially designed to deal with the kinds of stress that humans experience most often.

In everyday life, however, when we perceive some kind of threat, we often resort to the next level down, which is the superseded fight-or-flight mode. This is rarely an actual 'punch-up' or running for your life; it is a more subtle variation such as getting into an argument or avoiding the issue by changing the subject. If this kind of arousal is too frequent or prolonged the adverse effects of adrenalin are seen in high blood pressure and heart ailments.

The third alternative is worst of all; people can become so stressed that their minds shut down altogether due to the freeze response of the dorsal vagus system. Animals that do not have the new soothing ANS are more likely than us to die from the initial shock as can happen for a mouse when it is first caught by a cat. This is the last part of the nervous system to develop during pregnancy so babies that are born prematurely are at greater risk from any kind of stress in their early life and can die suddenly.

When stress has not been accommodated in some way there will be trauma, which is not simply a chemical imbalance in the brain. I can vouch for the fact that the most effective healing comes from whole body treatments such as exercise, yoga, massage, meditation and theatrical voice work, singing, dancing and loving social engagement. Van der Kolk pays tribute to Stephen Porges for the insights on which these kinds of treatment are based.

My book is not about major trauma, but the principles involved are relevant because we have all experienced some long-term effects of our experience of stress. These are part of who we are and they will shape the way we use our minds.

The function of our mind is to engage wisely and the experience of stress, even with its unpleasant feelings at times, is motivating us and guiding us in this direction. The very best example is the experience that we call love. It will always be stressful, but we could not do without it!

## Chapter 6

## What We Need Is Love

Love is number one. It's the most written about, sung about, thought about and desired feeling, emotion or state of mind. Poets can describe the nuances of the mind much more meaningfully than scientists do but even they have never explained love exhaustively. I'm sure there will always be more we will want to know about the experience that we call love. Why is it such a powerful yearning and how is it able to bring such great satisfaction to our being even though many things about it remain a mystery?

Our satisfaction alleviates our frustration but it is often the case that the exact nature of our frustration is hard to identify. I'm suggesting that the ultimate frustration is the demand for love. Shakespeare's *King Lear*, who unsuccessfully craves the complete love and devotion of his three daughters, is a classic case. If the greatest satisfaction comes from attending to our most fundamental need then there is a biological basis for love arising from our need to optimise both autonomy and connectedness. Left to themselves, reckless autonomy would destroy connectedness and unrestrained connectivity would eliminate our autonomous being. This is the basis for an unsentimental, scientific definition of love that Maturana gave us more than 30 years ago. It is probably only recently in our evolution that love came to be regarded as a virtue or enjoyed as romance. Before that it was already an indispensable part of the operation of the human mind.

Maturana defined love again recently as the 'fundamental sensory, operational and relational condition . . . that makes possible our human living.' [4] He used to say in lectures it was a relationship in which both I

---

[4] See an online paper by Humberto Maturana R., Ximena Dávila Y. and Simón Ramírez M. called *Cultural Biology: Systemic Consequences of Our Evolutionary Natural Drift as Molecular Autopoietic Systems* - DOI 10.1007/s10699-015-9431-1 *Found Sci.* (2015).

and the other could be the legitimate other (and I) at all times – the kind of coupling that conserves, and even enhances, our individual identities. Maturana emphasises the fact that will come out later in my story that seeing through eyes of love legitimises what we are seeing – only through love do we see clearly.

Amongst psychologists who have written about love my favourite is Erich Fromm whose book, *The Art of Loving*, is a classic in this field. He defines love as 'a union under the condition of preserving one's integrity.' He claims that, because our feelings of separateness are 'the source of shame . . . guilt and anxiety,' the connecting power of love is no less than 'the answer to the problem of human existence.' Those feelings of separateness that he said call for 'reunion by love' are built into our nature as living beings; they underpin our autonomy and compel our connectedness. What better way to define love than as the indispensable **facilitator of our fundamental tasks of being and belonging**?

We still have to deal with everyday stress so the ideal of a complete union or perfect love is unattainable – as it is also in poetry, philosophy and spirituality. At least having such an ideal shows us where to look for direction in our everyday experience of mind. I think the proper use of our mind boils down to *learning about love*. Our social engagement system is not a luxury we could do without – it is the most crucial element in our ability to stay alive in the first place and then cope with stress and enjoy the best possible feelings every day. We arrive in this world with an innate expectation of being loved and if we did not receive love in a practical way from the beginning we would not survive. Throughout our lives it remains our greatest need.

This is a biological fact so far as Maturana is concerned but I think it has another dimension also because of the mystery. Scientific explanation, on its own, robs our knowing of its most subtle beauty, which our imagination needs to flourish. It is love's *subjective* meaning that makes it such a recognisable part of our everyday experience. Being our most fundamental and unrequited yearning love is the epitome of mystery and never lets us forget our mind's relationship with the unknown. The lyrical Sam Keen, in *To Love and Be Loved*, says 'the problem of the meaning of life is solved in the mystery of love.' The mystery remains but at least we know in which direction to look to find meaning.

When I was trapped in those dark times I did not think I was loved and this is exactly what happens, once we are adults, if we look only to other people to tell us we are loved. When we are too dependent on our relationship with certain other people there is less space in our mind for broader connections or honest self-reflection. So where else could the feeling that you are loved come from? Love is such a fundamental need that we all experience it and we could not do without it yet its source remains a mystery. To put this another way we can say that *love seems to come from the unknown.* This is not science, of course; it is a personal belief. I believe in love because it is the kind of belief system that seems to me most necessary to fulfil our basic biological need for being and belonging and to legitimise what we see and do.

Although we experience love most strongly with another person the idea extends to all three kinds of relationships that I mentioned in Chapter 3 – with ourselves and with the unknown as well. Love is present before you know anything or have a particular person on whom to bestow it and it remains even after that person has gone away or died. I think it exists to support our aliveness. The poet and songwriter, Leonard Cohen, called it 'the only engine of survival.'

We can't say exactly what it is or where it comes from, yet we know that everything important to human beings is dependent upon love. Amongst many mysteries who can explain the fact that the more love you give away the more you seem to have in your life? Fortunately, we don't need to have an explanation for everything.

42

## Chapter 7

# Recognising the Unknown

We can choose to ignore the unknown but we can't really avoid its effect on our mind. It's all very well to know that our mind looks after our autonomy and our engagement as it deals with stress – and it needs love to do so. I still cannot know or control what the future has in store. Our attitude to this uncertainty makes a big difference to our feelings.

It is normal to hope for the best and assume all will be well but none of us is entirely happy about uncertainty. Some people handle it very badly. Another friend of mine, Fred, cannot commit to any invitation he receives because he worries that his chronic illness may prevent him from attending. A desire to predict the future is perhaps the most compelling tendency of the human mind, yet the need to know ahead of time what is going to happen is a major source of our anxiety.

Not knowing can be very useful yet it has become less and less popular in this day and age. We amaze ourselves with our ability to think up things to say to questions that probably warranted the simple answer: I don't know. As appointed experts or as parents it doesn't seem right to admit to not knowing. The individualism encouraged by our Western society entitles everyone to have a definite opinion about everything and to want to have a say in how things should be done. Historically there was more reliance on feelings of authority from outside ourselves provided by society or the church. These rules restricted individual freedom but they did make it easier to accept your place in the larger scheme of things. It was dangerous to question this authority as some famous dissenters discovered.

Progressive stages of 'enlightenment' and a growing enchantment with the scientific way of thinking brought more and more opportunities to question everything and to 'prove' how things work, often based on the simplistic assumption that effects have a simple linear cause, which they generally do not. The lure of apparent certainty was driven deep into our psyche and knowing the mechanism took precedence over accepting, or perhaps even admiring, the mystery. The problem is we don't actually understand things or **know what they mean** simply by knowing how they work. There is always something missing just as there was in my earlier life.

The philosopher Owen Barfield, who was one of 'the Inklings' at Oxford along with C.S. Lewis, J.R.R. Tolkien and others, posed an important question several decades ago: 'How is it that the more able man becomes to manipulate the world to his advantage, the less he can perceive any meaning in it? Exclusive emphasis on physical causes and effects involves a corresponding inattention to their meaning.' This is because everything our mind does is heavily dependent on the context.

The word, meaning, can be used in many ways; I refer to it as a subjective sense of satisfaction such that we feel we understand something. This wanes when the part of our mind that craves certainty and a feeling of knowing takes precedence over the part that sees a broader, more imaginative, perspective. Barfield echoed Goethe and others when he said that our imagination is required to apprehend the 'wholeness' in the specific details that we are observing such that we could obtain some meaning from them. This is paralleled in my experience by a recognition that there were larger-than-self goals as well as personal goals to consider – collective as well as individual responsibilities – and that this implied a subtle kind of larger-than-self 'authority.' This is a spiritual attitude that leads to some kind of faith, religious or otherwise.

Not knowing is more than the absence of knowing; it is an imaginative leap that recognises the unknown as a crucial component in the function of one's mind. Our feelings about the unknown are essential parts of our search for meaning and both love and faith are particular kinds of relationship with the unknown. Awareness of the unknown informs the known and enhances the mind, which becomes narrower and more simplistic without it. This is why finding the right question is often more important than knowing the answer. The answer always mirrors the question because it is trapped in the same thinking frame, which as we shall see is a characteristic of the operation of the left side of our brain.

The difference between the known and the unknown is like the difference between sound and silence. Another saving grace that helped my mind to cope with the dark times was that I was never afraid of silence. Growing up on a farm I kept to myself quite a lot. Other people I knew seemed to need constant sound; their radios or televisions blared wherever they were, they filled up every space in a conversation with words and they seemed to find silence disturbing. For many people there is no meaning to be found in silence; we speak of a stony silence, an awkward silence or a deathly silence. For a surprising number of people silence does not feel safe – it is a scary void.

Yet we also venerate silence in many ways; obviously in spiritual practices, also in music, language and in nature. Musicians revere silence because they know that the music is made by the space between the tones as much as by the tones themselves. The experience of a musical performance starts before the first note is played; amateurs are inclined to forget this and start too quickly while some famous maestros have kept their audience waiting for a few minutes before they began to play. The space between words that are spoken or sung is just as important as all good actors, comedians and orators understand very well; a singer such as Frank Sinatra had considerable effect through his phrasing of the words of a song. The silent bits are part of the feeling and whatever is deeply felt is a meaning likely to be shared with others. It takes the greatest skill to play the pauses well.

Our thinking and doing often becomes a rushing torrent in our mind and the ability to pause from time to time is a valuable and underrated asset. As well as providing respite it's a way of regaining a broader perspective, reconsidering the direction one is taking and tempering the mindless reactivity that can bring us undone. Management consultants such as Stephen Covey recommend leaving a space between the words someone says to you and the response that you make.

We live in a very noisy world, which is perhaps symptomatic of the ceaseless striving of our minds to try to know everything. I share with

Marcelo Gleiser and several other authors a favourite metaphor that likens knowledge to an island in an enormous sea. As he wrote in *The Island of Knowledge* the shoreline lengthens as knowledge grows so that our interface with the unknown gets bigger, not smaller, as we think we know more and more. I often feel that the more I have learned about something the less I seem to know.

I think it's our responsibility – and the challenge for our mind – to try to understand the context in every situation; I think that is the crux of our search for meaning. Cause-effect explanations tell us very little about the bigger picture within which this situation exists. Every decision, every new thought or action, is so heavily context-dependent that the logic of cause and effect is not nearly as useful as we often think it will be. Sometimes it is misleading because, unlike context, it misses the unknown altogether.

It seems to me that my subjective experience, which is essentially the flow of my feelings, is crucial for providing my sense of meaning. The purpose of objectivity in science is to discern the mechanism accurately, free from personal bias, which is indeed very useful. I have taken advantage of it often. A sense of meaning, however, is a personal experience – a property of the individual human mind. Biologists with a spiritual bent such as Charles Birch in *Science and Soul* allude to the process philosophy of Alfred North Whitehead in which it's suggested that subjectivity must necessarily take priority over objectivity. They say there is no reason to believe that other living things should not have a first-person perspective like we do – a predisposition to adapt, each according to its own needs, as I have explained about the biology of mind. It is this universal phenomenon that Andreas Weber likens to our experience of feelings in his *Biology of Wonder*.

Our feelings are the barometer of our being and belonging. The kind of meaning we obtain from our feelings is personal and imbued with whatever faith we have because it includes the unknown – yet it is also the reality of our experience. It cannot be expressed adequately in words, which Joseph Conrad said in his novel, *Under Western Eyes* are often 'the great foes of reality.' Our written explanations of anything do not do justice to the reality we experience, but fortunately, they can point us in that general direction.

In this book I have linked the phenomenon of love, which I regard as the ultimate mystery, to a recognition of the unknown. There is an association, particularly in poetry and in religious writing, between the unknown and what we call our *soul* – the most mysterious aspect of mind, perhaps. In the dark times I never really thought of having a soul and I did not feel loved. When I acknowledge my soul today I regard it as the part of me that seems to know, without fail, that I am loved, which is why I think of the unknown rather fondly! That has become my definition of the soul: *the place in your mind that knows you are loved*. The appreciation of beauty and the experience of awe and wonder are the kind of nourishment that the soul seems to need to grow and express itself.

## Chapter 8

# Hidden Mind

Our conscious mind is not capable of knowing everything that its subconscious partner is doing. We accept this and there is a good reason for it because we would only interfere with vital body functions in the same way you spoil your ability to ride a bike or even walk down the street if you think about it too much. The subconscious emotions contribute to our intelligence as I have said so it would be helpful to know something about their hidden influence, which is the subject of much psychological research.

Firstly, we can say that our perception is purposeful – we see what we see because of what we want and how we might act so our mind is essentially subjective and regulated by our feelings, thoughts and emotions at that time. This is why perception is so proactive and personal. It is not a passive process directed by what is out there – it is selective and is directed proactively from within according to our mental state at the time, which Henri Bortoft calls our 'organising idea' in his book *The Wholeness of Nature*. There would be far too much happening for us to take it all in anyway so the organising template, which is largely subconscious, directs our attention and even manipulates our sense organs using nerve fibres running to them from the brain. The mind is a connecting process, not a camera or a tape recorder.

Even though we see the world as we have shaped it with our mind, we can easily convince ourselves that this is the world 'as it really is' in which case everybody else should see it the same way. I believe it is written in the Talmud that 'we see the world as we are, not as it is.' William Blake fiercely defended the incredible world of his own imagination when he wrote: 'as a man is, so he sees.' Not recognising this is probably the most insidious hidden aspect of our mind and it leads to misunderstandings and futile kinds of arguments when two people simply have different versions of what happened.

In creating our stories we are lulled into thinking they are much more accurate and objective than they are. Firstly we simply don't remember the details as well as we think we do. In several famous experiments in which people wrote down where they were at a certain time (when the space shuttle blew up, for example) and were shown these notes a few years later, many of them vehemently denied what they had written because they now remembered it quite differently; a very small percentage remembered it exactly as they had written it. Secondly we have to fill in the many gaps in our stories from our imagination and these bits may not be true. Our story does not need to be entirely accurate or complete as long as it is internally consistent and fits reasonably well with our historical thread of meaning.

A Nobel prizewinning psychologist, Daniel Kahneman, in his best-selling book *Thinking Fast and Slow*, describes our 'experiencing self' and our 'remembering self' as two different parts of our mind. The latter is subject to various distortions including 'peak-end bias' whereby we tend to give more weight to the last thing that happened even though earlier events may have been more significant and 'duration neglect' whereby we forget how long things lasted though we remember other details. His research founded the field of behavioural economics, which is about the decision-making behaviour of consumers. He worked out the 'judgment heuristics' that we use subconsciously when making decisions, particularly about what to buy, and these are quite startling when they are pointed out.

He distinguishes two different kinds of thinking: the first (that he calls System 1) is automatic, rapid and intuitive, akin to the initial emotional response I am calling *affect*, and the second (that he calls System 2) is controlled, effortful and slow, more like the *story* we create. He concluded that although System 1 leads to many of our mistakes it is also the origin of most of the things we get right and he said that advances in cognitive science have shown us 'the marvels as well as the flaws in intuitive thinking.'

Another psychologist, Timothy Wilson, in an excellent book called *Strangers to Ourselves*, documents the important differences between what he calls our 'constructed self' and our 'adaptive unconscious.' The subconscious self is a pattern-detector rather than a fact-checker and it is faster and often automatic so it is more here-and-now than the conscious self will be. The constructed self is slower and more considered, but also more flexible and more sensitive to the positive whereas the unconscious is quite rigid and more sensitive to the negative. Thus our hidden mind is creating mental patterns without necessarily accommodating all the details, predisposing to a fixed position rather than flexibility and introducing a negative bias. Our conscious mind will counteract each of these and the combination of the two will constitute our next experience.

The idea of embodied cognition acknowledges the fact that the hidden influences that stem from our subconscious emotions are distributed throughout our whole body as well as our brain. Recent evidence for this includes the finding that holding a sad facial expression, or conversely a smile, changes the way you are feeling due to a change in your emotions. Sitting slouched in a chair compared to sitting up straight also leads to a corresponding change in your feelings and people who sat in a hard chair for a while were found to be more rigid and uncompromising in negotiations than when they had sat in a soft lounge chair. Physical exercise of any kind has a stimulating effect on your conscious mind.

Both our needs and our wants emanate from the hidden reaches of our mind and it is often difficult to distinguish one from the other as I know only too well. Eating and drinking are basic needs but my craving for chocolate and sweets is an example of wants that can take over your mind and lead you astray. Certain areas of the brain that are rich in dopamine receptors are known to be involved in pleasure-seeking and these become overactive in all forms of addiction.

When considering one's own bad habits it is always consoling to find somebody else who is worse than you are and I have to say that Alastair fits the bill in that regard. He stocks up big with sweet things for a future occasion, then ends up eating them all before the day is out! The fact is that undesirable habits like these are usually impossible to change just by thinking about them. This is where the power of the hidden mind comes in because it is only by *doing* things differently that your mind gradually changes as we shall see.

I've often wondered, if our feelings are so useful, why do they lead us astray with misplaced wanting. If you've ever ordered another cheeseburger only to discover when it came that you no longer want it, you have experienced what Timothy Wilson and Daniel Gilbert call 'miswanting.' They researched the inaccuracy with which our minds predict the future. We imagine the future based on our feelings right now and when the future arrives we will probably have a different set of feelings so we often get it wrong. Of course the hidden influences of our mind also include commonsense and prudence based on previous experience which will help us to make good decisions too.

Sometimes our conscious mind is trying too hard and we slip up because this deprives us of the 'marvels' of our intuition. Conversely, a brilliant footballer weaving his way across the field or a sculptor like Michelangelo revealing the beauty he had already seen within the marble block, are employing what the Chinese call *wu-wei*. They are 'in the zone' and tapping into subconscious knowing without thinking about it at all. In a book called *Trying Not To Try*, Edward Slingerland gives us some insight into this mysterious process. He said the two key elements of it are a complete lack of self-consciousness and an awareness of working within something larger-than-self – aspects of mind that are central to the story I am telling.

An unfortunate consequence of underestimating the hidden mind is that we think we know ourselves better than we really do. Wilson cites an amusing example from George Bernard Shaw's play *Pygmalion*. Henry Higgins sees himself as a gracious, fair-minded, cultured gentleman whereas he is actually prideful, misogynous, controlling and often quite crude. When his housekeeper Mrs Pierce chastises him for swearing and using his nightgown as a napkin he tells his friend Pickering that he cannot understand how she could so misrepresent him. When Mrs Pierce said he uttered swear words to 'his boots, the butter and the brown bread' he replied '. . . mere alliteration, Mrs Pierce, natural to a poet.'

It can be amusing to notice someone else's blind spots, but what about one's own? In my dark period I had a jaundiced view of what other people thought about my behaviour and I was also too self-conscious to see anything from another person's viewpoint. As the veil of my selfishness lifted I began to see a broader perspective, but I still found it difficult to give up some habitual behaviours even though I knew they were objectionable. Our most established habits are the hardest to see and the pattern-loving nature of our hidden mind maintains its hold on you whether that habit is good for you or not. We will revisit this problem later after we take a closer look at the emotions, feelings and thoughts themselves and the way they enable our social engagement and sharing of meaning.

## Chapter 9

# Emotions, Feelings and Thoughts

We enjoy eating a delicious meal without necessarily being able to recognise the individual ingredients that are in it. It's the same with our experience of mind yet we also know that emotions, feelings and thoughts each contribute something different to the combined effect.

The best way I know to see the huge influence that **emotions** have is to think of them as *the doings of the subconscious mind* – even though many of their effects do become noticeable over time. This is a big generalisation, but a useful one. All the hormonal and nervous patterns of connection within our body and brain are a swirling tide of *affect* that we recognise only in its consequences, not in its actual happening. As I said earlier, emotions are the primary experience, the leading edge of our mind. There is good physiological evidence for this from researchers like Antonio Damasio, whose books include *The Feeling of What Happens*. Benjamin Libet in the 1970's and others since then showed that appropriate subconscious changes in the brain precede a conscious thought or action by at least half a second. You can consciously change your mind, of course, by interrupting this process, but your next actions or words still have to be generated subconsciously.

So even though we can change direction via our actions and thoughts, we are mostly living in the wake of our emotional swirl. It predisposes rather than directs what our mind is doing. For example an emotion of fear might concentrate our attention in certain ways whereas joyful anticipation might open it up to more opportunities. Damasio invented a psychological card game that came to be called the Iowa Gambling Task in which players either won or lost money when they chose a card from one of four different decks. Some decks paid more consistently than others and players with healthy brains soon identified these, on a hunch at first, before they put it into words. We often say we had a feeling about something before it became a thought. The telling point is that people with damage to emotion-generating areas of the brain could not do this. It took longer for reason to figure it out if the emotional intelligence was lacking.

***Feelings*** are not the same as emotions in that they are a *conscious awareness* that we have of our experience that is non-verbal in the first instance. We often think of them as emotions or turn them into thoughts but I want to draw attention to what is different about them. I am suggesting that the feeling occupies some middle ground between the two. It lacks the logic and detail of a thought but it can be identified in our experience directly, unlike the emotion. It also affects what we say and do and it plays a far bigger role than we generally realise in the way we make meaning.

To give feelings their identity we have to blend the known with the unknown, which is actually not unusual for our mind – we do it all the time. Things we don't know and can't know intrude into our sense of meaning as it is formed anew in each moment. The words we use for our story are commentaries on our experience, not the experience itself. What characterises feelings is the sense that part of the experience can't quite be explained in words – when you try to do that something seems to have been lost.

Hidden parts of the mind cause us to say things we 'didn't mean to say' or do things we 'didn't mean to do' from time to time. The philosopher Laurent Dubreuil proposes in his book, *The Intellective Space – Thinking Beyond Cognition,* that there is a distinct mental process whereby we 'say more than we think and think more than we say' and by acknowledging this we will understand our mind better. He doesn't recognise the traditional dichotomy between cognition and emotion, suggesting that it is their combined effect that produces meaning and that this is inadequately captured in language, which he says is 'opaque' and betrays us to some extent. I think the role of our feelings is implied in his explanation.

Feelings are shy and elusive because they lose their identity as they are fashioned into thoughts or they are so vague they slip back into the subconscious swirl. But they are always there, attached to both our thoughts and our emotions. Mary E. Clark wrote in her book, *In Search of Human Nature*, that 'perhaps it is the quintessential error of the modern Western world-view to suppose that thought can occur without feeling.' We do this because thought assumes a pre-eminent position at the 'head' of our mind, as distinct from the 'heart.' While this is valuable in many ways, it has led us astray as the main guiding principle for the use of our mind.

Our ***thoughts*** can be vague and haphazard too although they pride themselves on being logical and unambiguous most of the time. Because this kind of language is so helpful for the interpersonal communication that we need to achieve things together we have constructed a view of reality that is one step removed from our actual experience. In this dual reality there are two kinds of meaning: firstly, what this situation is supposed to mean, objectively and logically, and secondly, what it actually means as part of one's experience. In other words there is a third-person and a first-person perspective. Words all have dictionary meanings attached to them but as we are using them we are creating personal meanings based on our own experience.

For making meaning our feelings are crucial because they tell us what is important – what matters. As Paul Gilbert says in his delightful book, *Stumbling on Happiness*, 'feelings don't just matter, they are what mattering means.' Without a feeling about something it simply wouldn't have any significance – it wouldn't be of concern to you so it would mean nothing – even if the cold logic of language suggested otherwise. To encode meaning solely in the language is to disembody cognition and place it outside human experience. Because the feelings occupy a space between the thoughts and the emotions, both of which may take them over, the more subtle feelings are easily missed. Yet 'feelings are what matter most in life' as the distinguished biologist, Charles Birch, puts it in his book called *Feelings*.

In our everyday experience it's obvious that feelings are at the forefront, though they are not acting alone. Our social life revolves around the people and places that make us feel good. Our consumer society is fuelled by advertising which is directed at our feelings. Whether it is a breakfast cereal, a soft drink or a motor car, the ads don't need to tell you much about the product because their emphasis is the simple message: *'what a feeling!'* Successful products usually have extra ingredients such as scent, froth or fizz that contribute nothing except a nice feeling when you use them. People are more likely to buy services that make them feel good and the house you buy will be justified by location and resale value but it will almost certainly be the one that feels right.

However, thought promotes the idea that it knows best and deserves to stand above feelings or emotions as the leader of our mind. Given our cultural history for the last several hundred years this is only to be expected. We emerged from the 'dark ages' by developing our 'intellect' while religions and philosophy combined to distance us from animal passion and take the higher moral ground. An awesome human creativity was unleashed in art, literature, music, cathedrals and cities. The advent of science brought unprecedented advances in our mechanisation and lifestyle. Then the digital age made information seem more important than meaning and the computer became the sadly inappropriate metaphor for understanding the brain as if it was mechanical rather than biological. The idea of embodied cognition now restores some balance to this story without denying the great power of thought.

Thought is not precise like the operation of a computer because the language we use has quite different properties from the language that computers use. It is constructed from a great many different metaphors, analogies and images over a long period of time. Unsurprisingly, the most common origin of these metaphors is our experience of the physical world and of our bodies. We say we are up when we feel good and down when we feel bad, on top of things when we're successful or behind when we're running late, utilising metaphors from space and time. We go to the head of the table or the heart of the matter, know things in our bones, prick up our ears, feel our skin crawl or grow queasy at the thought.

In a more general sense we can say that conscious thoughts originate as an unfurling of shapes and patterns that have formed within our body. A simple way of understanding how emotions shape our mind is the idea that patterns of internal connectivity become the patterns for our relationships with our world. In *Intelligence in the Flesh*, Guy Claxton describes how our abstraction of meaning is rooted in bodily movement – reaching conclusions, grasping the idea, picking things up, getting and giving – because our being involves doing. This relationship between emotions and reason is imprecise and approximate so that our thoughts may be only a pale reflection of the deeper meaning. Often they are more concerned with the social circumstances at that time.

Imprecise meaning or fuzziness is actually essential for our minds to do their job. We could not connect as well as we do with other people if our language was more accurate because there would not be sufficient overlap of individual meanings for us to achieve a sense of shared meaning. Saying that my life is like a 'can of worms' may explain more than if I were to list the details. The pattern-seeking nature of our subconscious mind enables us to build bridges between one image and another in our metaphors. Without 'fuzzy logic' a consensus could never be achieved and the essential business of our conversation would not thrive.

That would be a devastating loss because conversation is the process whereby we create our culture or design the way we choose to live together. Every day we create our individual stories and share these with other people and this is the way our culture evolves, for better or for worse. Our culture is the thread of meaning for our community, as one's story is for the individual. The feelings that accompany our thoughts contribute more to this meaning than we usually admit. Alfred North Whitehead was one who recognised this when he described thoughts as 'intellectualised feelings.'

When your friend arrives to visit she might tell you part of her story: her car had a flat tyre so she caught the train, which was running late, and then it started raining and the taxi driver put her out in a puddle – it's a wonder she got here at all! The story is built around her feelings. On the other hand when a scientist or a businessman describes something he regards as important he will make it sound dispassionate and reasoned to give it more 'weight' and we will all pretend there is no emotion behind it and no feelings involved. Sometimes the feelings are all too obvious such as when I had forgotten to pass on a telephone message to my wife,

Penelope, causing her to miss an important appointment and she made it very clear that she was feeling angry! I felt bad about it too.

The agents that cause our feelings can be identified but not the exact cause of any particular feeling. They are shaped firstly by our emotions (some inborn, some learned), secondly by our thinking, which can overwhelm everything else at times, and thirdly by the sensory stimuli affecting us at that time. In a book called *Embodied: The Psychology of Physical Sensation,* Christopher Eccleston identified 15 different senses that influence our feeling state. We are most aware of the sights, sounds, smells, taste and touch that our special sense organs bring to our attention but our mind is also busy maintaining body processes so hunger, fatigue, pain, itch, heat and cold and the vital proprioceptive senses whereby we keep our balance and move about are also playing their part.

The bemusing thing about feelings is that they are always yours and you are never without them but they seem to have a life of their own in that you didn't choose them; they arrived of their own accord. You have little control over them though it's reported to be easier to make yourself sad than it is to make yourself happy. Christophe André, in a book called *Feelings and Moods,* calls them the 'internal echoes' of what is happening and 'the beating heart of our link with the world' and he adds an important rider – that they make us 'more lucid.'

We like to label them as good or bad, from a basic instinct to distinguish an opportunity from a threat but in reality they can be both. In all languages there are more words for negative feelings than for positive ones and psychological tests show we are quicker to detect the negative ones from a list of words flashed on a screen. Balancing this is the fact that we can explain the positive feelings more comfortably when we reflect on them so positive moods generally predominate in the longer term. As I said before, our instinctive and subconscious mind is geared for a quick reaction to trouble while the more reflective, distinctly human, part of our mind is designed to promote feelings of wellbeing.

Negative feelings lead towards withdrawal and avoidance, perhaps irritation, while positive feelings promote openness and accessibility along with curiosity and enthusiasm. The negative ones are put into language more slowly with more detail and a narrower outlook while good feelings take hold quickly and expansively making us more energetic and persuasive, though their wider generalisation can also be misleading.

We often have more than one feeling at the same time and it's interesting that the good and the bad can occur together; sadness doesn't entirely prevent joy from popping up, for example. There can be a rich, multi-coloured or multi-flavoured mix of feelings. Feelings also have a property called remanence, which means they can persist after the initial cause has long passed. Getting stuck in a feeling is referred to as a mood, which affects our behaviour and our relationships.

Accepting every feeling – allowing it to be there when it occurs, trusting that it will morph into another one – is the unmistakeable sign of a healthy mind. The practice known as mindfulness meditation helps with this. It usually begins with a deliberate relaxation of the body, region by region. As the body relaxes so does the mind. Then it's possible – often by focussing on your breathing – to be much more in the present moment than we normally are. We are often missing the most authentic part of our experience by taking refuge somewhere other than in our current feelings. Christophe André makes an important distinction between *rumination*, a self-centred, blaming and judgmental kind of reflection, and a genuine *reflection* that is open-minded and accepting and therefore allows for moving on instead of staying in the problem.

The best-selling author and social researcher, Brené Brown, in her books like *Rising Strong* and *The Gifts of Imperfection* and her much-acclaimed TED talk on *The Power of Vulnerability*, calls this essential process of being with your feelings the 'reckoning' and the 'rumble.' She gives examples from her own life of what happens if she tries to avoid honest self-examination and why it is important to check out one's story to detect the lies it may contain. Her phrase 'wholehearted living' captures the idea of our whole body as our mind. We can't really manage our feelings because we don't have that kind of control over them but we do need to own and respect them and make them welcome.

Equating the emotions with our subconscious as I've done belies their tremendous influence as the underlying framework of our mind. An emotion can overcome each of our three strongest motivations: hunger, sex and the will to live. People will go without food altogether if they find it too disgusting, are easily put off having sex by some interfering emotion and can take their own lives while in the grip of the deepest despair. Those primary motivations are themselves the healthy products of emotion. At their best the emotions lay the solid foundation for a satisfied mind. There are three ways they can go wrong: an emotion can occur with the wrong intensity (*e.g.* excessive anger) or the wrong expression (*e.g.* silence for expressing anger) or it can simply be the wrong emotion for that situation (*e.g.* fear that is unfounded).

Such is the power of the emotional pattern formed at the deepest level of our mind that we often have cause to doubt whether our thinking is in control. The process is likened to riding an elephant by Jonathan Haidt, an American psychologist who wrote *The Happiness Hypothesis*. Our thinking and will is the mahout or elephant rider who guides the much more powerful elephant by subtle nudges based on his or her acute awareness of every slight movement they make together and what it signifies for achieving what they want to achieve. Without this skill, which takes years to develop, your elephant could take you on a dangerous and bumpy ride and you could not prevent this from happening. We use our awareness of feelings to integrate thought and emotions.

The way we distinguish one emotion from another has mostly been based on their outward expression. Charles Darwin's book, *The Expression of the Emotions in Man and Animals*, was the starting point well over a century ago. When an American psychologist, Paul Ekman, showed in the 1960's that facial expressions for several common emotions were recognised across different cultures, these became widely accepted as the universal human emotions – happiness, sadness, fear, anger, disgust and surprise. One of Ekman's books, *Emotions Revealed*, describes his further refinement of facial expression as an accurate indicator of many other emotions. But the list of different emotions can go on and on and people disagree about what they should be called. The emotion that people say they desire most, happiness, is so multi-faceted and subjective that it is difficult to define.

Naming the emotions can be simplified by following the thinking of Jaak Panksepp as it is summarised in his book with Lucy Biven called *The Archaeology of Mind – Neuroevolutionary Origins of Human Emotions*. Panksepp is an Estonian-born neuroscientist working in America with whom I feel an affinity because he works with animals to understand the evolution of our human emotions. He identified seven distinct neural networks in the brain that each produce one of our *primary instinctual emotions*. We are born with these, as are other mammals, and they are the foundations for all our other emotions, which are variations we have learned in the course of our lifetimes, especially in the first few years. We tend to think of guilt and shame, jealousy and envy, resentment, contempt and even anxiety and depression as innate elements of our emotional repertoire that could not be changed, but it's more useful to think of them as learned derivatives of the primary set of emotional instincts. Panksepp's seven primary emotions that I have renamed slightly are *seeking, fear, anger, grief, lust, care* and *play*.

The first one, **seeking**, is quite new to the emotion scientist's lexicon and it is clearly the most fundamental and far-reaching in its effects. It could be compared to the deep yearning we all feel that the poet, John O'Donohue, calls 'an undertow of possibility.' It is felt in the excitement of exploring and discovering, pursuing and realising our expectations, and it is driven by the fact that everything is changing and we must always be trying to adapt. It is our motivation to engage, not just for survival, but in new ways that our imagination suggests might be more interesting and better for our wellbeing. Seeking is a pleasure in itself; it is probably the main source of pleasure and therefore of happiness, which is why happiness is not really a destination – it's a pleasing aspect of the journey.

The identification of a 'pleasure' or 'reward' centre in the brain was a major milestone in $20^{th}$ century neuroscience, but also a false lead. The brain networks in which the neurotransmitter, dopamine, is especially active that cause insatiable 'pleasure seeking' in rats when they are stimulated are now known to fire in advance of and in *anticipation* of rewards; in other words they are an expectation and checking system rather than a satisfaction system. They are implicated in all our addiction traps. This is one of the reasons that happiness seems to be found more easily by striving for something else that is meaningful rather than chasing it directly.

***Fear*** is an obvious consequence of seeking because we are sure to come across threats as well as opportunities. We have a great need for this emotion as a motivator and it serves us by sharpening our intellectual focus and our intuitive reflexes; without fear the mind gets lazy. Its main derivative, anxiety, is an expectation of fear that we learn throughout our lives, which narrows our attention and sabotages our desire to love. In today's world there are so many distractions and interruptions that we carry a lot of unfinished business and it's common to be feeling that there must be something more I need to do (called the Zeigarnik effect).

***Anger*** stems from an impulse to correct something you perceive to be wrong and, while it can protect one's autonomy at times, the learned variations of it such as resentment can be a serious blight for one's mind. These emotions and the range of negative feelings that derive from them will be considered in Chapter 15 as components of our suffering.

***Grief*** is the distress and pain of separateness that is most apparent after the loss of a loved one. Panksepp uses the word, panic, because separation produces agitated behaviour, but he also makes it clear that this is not the same as the fear response; it is a quite different deep instinct arising from our craving for connectedness. We often underestimate the need for grieving after any kind of separation or moving on, even a minor one.

***Lust***, our natural sexual desire, is not simply for reproduction because sexual intimacy is a very satisfying component of our social engagement. It also manifests as greed in other ways – selfishly wanting more of everything – which can happen when sexual impulses get confused with other desires for power and control. Panksepp also gave consideration to disgust as a deep-seated emotion, but he considered its cultural variation to be primarily learned.

***Care*** and ***play*** are the emotions from which our quintessentially human behaviours arise. The physical contact of hugging and touching are indispensable for our mind and, as I said, the mother-baby bond is the template for caring behaviour and the foundation stone for our ability to love. In my book love is not a primary emotion. I agree with Karla McLaren who wrote *The Language of Emotions* that love is something more than an emotion because it exists whether you and I have feelings about it or not. We are attracted to it and it guides us from the depths of our mind and works wonders for us if we believe in it and cultivate it but it is not just another component of our emotional repertoire.

We share the ability to play with many other animals and we retain it more obviously into our adulthood and have refined it a great deal. Far from being a trivial accompaniment, it is one of the pillars of the human mind. Stuart Brown explains in his book, *Play*, how it 'shapes the brain, opens the imagination and invigorates the soul.' Panksepp features it for its association in the brain with seeking and pleasure. The important learned emotions that derive from care, lust, play and seeking will be elaborated further as we explore everyday love in more detail. They constitute great pleasures and many different kinds of sorrow and pain.

I have emphasised the role of feelings because I think they are the cutting edge of our mind's work although they could not do it on their own. Regarding autonomy, they help us to know ourselves. When E. E. Cummings wrote a *Poet's Advice to Students* he said that it's very hard to write anything original and he added: 'Whenever you think, or you believe, or you know, you're a lot of other people; but the moment you feel, you're nobody-but-yourself . . .' Regarding connectedness, feelings provide the authenticity we need to connect most effectively with other people. Sharing our success stories can be fun, but the strongest connections we make are through our stories of vulnerability and hardship.

What shapes our feelings most effectively is our interaction with the minds of others. Christophe André said our feelings serve to make our minds more 'lucid,' which means that we can see more clearly. What we see is not the selfish pride of being in control and knowing a lot but rather the vulnerability of being a single living unit situated in a vast unknown, thankfully, along with lots of other people. And as Brené Brown illustrates powerfully in her work, to become aware of our vulnerability is actually the source of our strength. The background of our emotions informs us of our neediness, reminding us of all the things we can't control and revealing our lack of self-sufficiency. Our feelings and thoughts build on that so we can do what we have to do.

We now turn to the way that emotions, feelings and thoughts combine in our incredible social engagement.

## Chapter 10

## The Magic of Social Engagement

There are many apparent differences between mankind and other animals, notably the language we use and the way we use it, yet in the careful analysis of Thomas Suddenhorf in his book, *The Gap – The Science of What Separates Us from Animals*, the salient differences boil down to just two: our apparently limitless imagination and an 'insatiable drive to link our minds together.' Most researchers agree that our much larger brain came about as we formed bigger social groups and refined our interpersonal behaviours into the exquisite social engagement system that we have today.

Our faces and our hands are unique and special. The human species is noted for its neoteny, which means that we stay younger for much longer than other animals do. We don't grow thick hair or hide as we mature; we retain the soft sensitive skin and the facial flexibility of children, along with the ability to play, throughout our lives. Our evolving need for intimate connectedness carried with it the vulnerability and sensitivity that makes us human.

The most obvious advanced feature of our hands is that they can manipulate things more precisely and in that sense they parallel our mind. Our hands have always been central to our feelings of competence because we use them to make things, which young children still love doing, but adults get to do less often nowadays. Our being arises from our doing so the linkage between our hands and brain has shaped our minds powerfully throughout its evolution and the different ways we use our hands today are gradually altering our minds.

Whatever you do with your hands attracts attention – if you put them near something other people notice. We use our hands very deliberately for connecting, in a handshake for example; a mother might hold and admire her baby's little hand and a visiting relative might take one baby finger and move it about as if to say: you're one of us. But the greatest thing about our hands was pointed out by Maturana and his colleague Gerda Verden Zöller. They are the ultimate organ of caress because they are soft and we can shape them to any part of the human body; this ability was significant for developing our humanness. Body contact and the loving caress, including massage, are powerful forms of connectedness for humans.

We crave to connect, often without realising it. We have a mind that is disposed towards interpreting the emotions and feelings of others and arranging ourselves accordingly. When we spend time together this happens subconsciously as well as consciously. I like to add to the metaphor of the subconscious as an elephant that it is good to park your elephant with others of its kind so they can make 'elephant talk' because it is often useful for steadying one's mind to simply be in the company of other people.

Our faces and eyes are the windows through which we see one another's feelings. The human face has 43 sets of muscles and Paul Ekman and his colleagues documented 64 different expressions in their Facial Action Coding System. You only have to look at the emoticons we use today to appreciate our fascination with a face. Edgar Allen Poe used to imagine and copy the facial expression of his characters to help him work out what he would have them do or say next in his stories.

I have said that we engage with one another most powerfully through our vulnerability and there is no stronger connecting influence than the uniquely human experience of crying and the anguished facial expression that crying entails. No other animal sheds tears in this way though some show the anguish in their behaviour. We probably need to cry as Michael Trimble points out in his book, *Why Humans Like to Cry*, and it does seem to alleviate our stress somewhat unless it is especially despairing and prolonged. It is associated with the release of calming hormones such as endorphins.

Just as powerful, but more aligned with positive feelings, are the extraordinary human behaviours of smiling and laughing. The comedian, Milton Berle, called laughter an 'instant vacation' and Maturana called it a 'momentary respite' because of the way it interrupts whatever your mind is doing and releases tension. Breathing out or sighing slows your heartbeat and a hearty laugh is a strong and spontaneous release of breath. We usually need the company of other people to be able to laugh in this way. Again there are relaxing hormones involved and apparent benefits for our immune system and our health.

The smile is the most incredible connecting device of all. It can be seen from 50 metres away (further than any other expression), which is about the distance you could throw a spear if smiling was the last thing on your mind. Seeing your baby's first 'smile' is an unforgettable experience. Even though it is an innate instinct at that stage and even occurs in the womb, it is a powerful connection that soon becomes meaningful in subtle ways; adult smiles vary in their meaning too. In the 19th century a French neuroanatomist called Duchenne reported that there were two different kinds of smile: one in which the involuntary muscle under and around the eye (the orbicularis oculi) was involved and another in which it was not. These came to be known as D-smiles and non-D-smiles.

What is extraordinary is that we are all sensitive enough to tell the difference between a genuine smile and one that is manufactured and to recognise, at least subconsciously, whether facial expressions are authentically related to a feeling or not. Even though the physical changes are very small we specialise in being able to read one another's feelings by watching faces. It's been found, at least for smiles, that we do this by unconsciously mimicking the other person's expression for a moment. Experiments showed that simply holding a pencil between your lips so as to prevent your face smiling interfered with this process. People who had received Botox to paralyse facial muscles were found to have lost some of their ability to recognise the emotions of others. An associated finding that their clinical depression had improved was said to be because their less worried facial expression now triggered fewer negative feelings.

This is a telling example of the powerful linkage between the face and the mind and between two people in the course of social engagement. The significance of facial expression is partly because many of these tiny muscles are not under voluntary control, especially those around the eyes and the corner of the lips, so your face may be telling more about how you are feeling than you realise. These involuntary muscles are linked to the ANS through the brain stem so they are involved in every stress response and every subtle connection that we make with one another, which is where the strategic management of stress by means of social engagement comes into play.

The ANS has both a *motor* function, causing the muscle contractions in our face and elsewhere, and a *sensory* function being its ability to monitor the changes in our organs and our internal state, which is why the opportunity to connect with another person is so helpful in managing stress. The ANS affects our voice and our hearing that are also vital elements of social engagement. The arousing ANS, driven by adrenalin, expresses any kind of excitement you feel, not just fight or flight, which affects your connectedness. Feelings of fear produce a knot in your stomach and a pounding heart. There is good evidence that we detect fear in one another by our sense of smell so all the senses are involved.

The *new soothing ANS* (or ventral vagus system) that I described in Chapter 5 plays a crucial role through its effect on your heartbeat. It is the main slowing mechanism for your heart, which is set at a higher rate by the arousing ANS through the 'pacemaker' node and then fine-tuned by the waxing and waning of what is called the 'vagal brake.' The more healthy and fit you are the better this works and there is a measure of it called Heart Rate Variability or HRV. This is not quite what you might think; it's actually the desired slight difference in heartrate between the in-breath (when your heart speeds up) and the out-breath (when your heart slows down). It's a small difference, only detectable by instruments like an ECG machine, but it's worth measuring because it has been found that people with a high HRV cope better with stress and have better attention control. Low HRV has been associated with some chronic illnesses, anxiety disorders and depression.

When we say we feel the effects of social engagement in our heart more than our head we are not just speaking figuratively! In Eastern languages the same word is often used for heart and mind because it is assumed that they work closely together. Early Western philosophers identified the mind more closely with the heart than with the brain, which Aristotle thought was merely a cooling device for the blood. And there is an alternative field of medicine concerned with heart waves that seem to interact with the brain.

You know from experience that your heart will skip a beat as you catch sight of your new lover approaching. A loving relationship is stressful in the sense that your mind must work hard to keep adjusting the connectedness, but it is the healthiest kind of stimulation of all and also the one we can least do without. The everyday experience we call *love* is not optional for human beings – it is essential for our survival.

Human babies are born with less brain development and fewer physical skills than the young of any other species and our brain will only develop properly if we receive love. There are documented cases of children who survived being raised by wild animals but they failed to develop a human way of thinking. Also there are famous studies in orphanages where babies were deliberately deprived of social interaction, and also restricted in their movement, to the great detriment of their mind in later life. The baby's mind is not pre-formed at birth; it has to be shaped by its history of social interaction in which feelings will lead the way.

A world authority on child development, Peter Hobson, wrote in his book, *The Cradle of Thought*, that 'the tools of thought are constructed on the basis of the infant's emotional involvement with other people.' Long before the meanings are put into words it is *an exchange of actions and feelings* and this continues to be the core of all our social engagement, though as adults we may not be aware that this is what is happening. From the beginning the baby learns the difference between humans and things and the important differences between one human and another. A little later she (or he) learns to notice and be influenced by what her caregiver thinks and feels about something before she acts herself and then, after a while, that it could be preferable *not* to take notice of what her parent thinks when she wants to really be herself! The tension between being and belonging fuels the operation of one's mind throughout life.

The baby's brain networks develop rapidly as new connections, called synapses, are formed according to his or her experience, which is why loving interaction is so necessary. From about age three until puberty is the peak period for forming new patterns in the brain and altering them rapidly. The adolescent years are especially important for the development of our minds because there is a pruning and prioritising of brain networks according to the way the mind is being used. This continues into the twenties after which there is still plasticity available to the brain although it has reached a fairly stable pattern that best suits your particular lifestyle.

Social engagement is not possible unless we feel safe, especially when it involves hugging and close physical contact. We have an innate subconscious mechanism that checks for danger when other people are close by so we always need some reassurance from faces and hands, voice and posture, to enable our physiology to establish an intimate relationship. This is the 'immobilisation without fear' that Stephen Porges refers to as the foundation of our experience of love.

The hormone, oxytocin, is also involved. A leading oxytocin researcher is Sue Carter – Stephen Porges' wife. She showed that this hormone that is released to aid childbirth and milk letdown and also during sexual intercourse has the beneficial effect of calming fear, increasing confidence and promoting strong pair-bonding. So the feelings generated in couples as their social engagement becomes more intimate and more physical naturally lead those people towards long-term monogamous relationships. Oxytocin loosens brain networks that promote individuality and strengthens those that foster mutuality so it is a great boon for our mind's work of developing successful relationships. Having a lot of casual sex might be confusing for the developing brain in this regard.

Part of the romantic pleasure of love is seduction, which is a fine balance between the excitement that mild fear generates and the safe confident feelings of love – another of the balancing marvels of our mind performed for us by our ANS. Sexual intercourse is a powerful component of healthy social engagement, but if it is used to exploit another person it causes great harm to the mind. Rape, especially of children, is traumatic in the extreme because of the enormous sensitivity of the physiological and psychological trust involved in love.

In everyday experience social engagement doesn't always work in a thoroughly pleasant way. The magic can disappear completely when your feelings become a dislike for another person and instead of attraction there could be extreme anger or revulsion, such is the natural power of this process. Self-consciousness takes over and the connecting part of the equation goes out the window for the time being. This can also happen in a more insidious way through our moods.

When feelings are sustained for longer than a few minutes they become moods and they affect our personal interactions through the meaning generated in our feelings. Moods are very important modulators of our social engagement, particularly when there is a negative or defensive aspect to them. In that case they cause the connection to lose authenticity and become uncomfortable and then our stories start to include more lies such as 'he doesn't like me because I'm not pretty' or 'she doesn't think I'm doing the right thing.'

I like the metaphor of a jazz band as a way of thinking about our connectedness through feelings and moods. A good musician is aware of the tempo and the notes he is playing, which become his feelings and his 'mood,' and he is also aware of the larger pattern of rhythm, harmony and chord progression that includes the other musicians. If he is not listening attentively to the connectedness of the band as a whole the music will fall apart. Moods can become selfish preoccupations but if you remember the larger-than-self needs of the 'band' and you want to 'make music,' your moods can form creative combinations with the moods of others and start to flow in the direction that leads towards a love song.

My friend Alastair still figures in my life. In the years since I started writing this book he has come out of himself a bit more through experiencing more social engagement. He met a woman whose story overlapped with his own and she brought a larger circle of friends and acquaintances into his life. Then I noticed that he gradually sabotaged this relationship with his negativity and so he has gone back to living alone. We still talk about these things from time to time and he seems a bit more willing to entertain my ideas about the importance of connectedness so I remain hopeful that he will get some relief from his 'bondage of self' one day as he gets to experience more of what I call shared meaning.

## Chapter 11

# Shared Meaning

Our daily experience is rife with misunderstandings. A close friend thought I was angry with her about something she had done whereas I was actually upset at losing a valuable file from my computer. At other times I misunderstood suggestions that she made to me. These are trivial examples; more serious misunderstandings can poison relationships over a period of time if they are not detected.

Many people don't realise that the meaning that is formed in one's mind cannot be transferred directly to another person's mind. Each individual's mind can be influenced by outside forces, but at its core it has to manage itself to be autonomous so it is a semantically-closed unit. Whatever I am saying here came from my meaning-making process but what it means to you is entirely your business. We tend to assume that what I meant is what you understood, which could only happen if our minds were running identical flow patterns at that time. This is highly improbable, though a bit more likely if we have a lot of history in common.

Yet we must achieve meaningful connections in order to survive so we are blessed with this 'insatiable drive to link our minds together' that is our social engagement system. The fact that I can't receive your exact meaning, nor transmit mine to you, makes us feel lonely. What we can do is try to find some meaning that we can share. Of course I pick up many hints from the words you use because they have a standard set of meanings assigned to them, but the fact is that I still construct my own version and what we share is only the bit where my version overlaps with yours. This shared meaning is the glue that melds our individual stories into the collective mind that is our society.

We generally regard our everyday conversation as a rather mundane 'bread-and-butter' affair, but in fact it is an essential part of the core business of our mind. Simply talking with another person activates all our mind's physiological processes throughout the body and brain, particularly our ANS because it involves our eyes and ears, tongue, mouth and face. What we see in another's face and hear in another's voice and what we express in return shapes each new moment of our lives. Some of the involuntary muscles also affect our hearing, which therefore varies according to our feelings; we are naturally better at hearing what we like to hear and sometimes we don't hear at all (as you probably know if you have your own children!)

In a book called *Time to Converse*, Alan Stewart has written about different modes of conversation, pointing out that argument, debate and discussion are not the same as open non-judgmental conversing that is guided by mutual respect and by his motto that we simply aim to 'treat each other well.' The physicist, David Bohm, promoted a particular form of dialogue that he said tapped 'a pool of common meaning' and the practice known as Appreciative Enquiry aims to 'ignite the collective imagination.' An English philosopher, Theodore Zeldin, who founded the Oxford Muse, pointed out in his book, *Conversation*, that conversation changes the way we see the world and then it changes the world. Maturana also explained that our culture is created through our conversation.

Shared meaning is especially important in the workplace where it is more objective because we need the logic of language to coordinate our individual actions to get things done. Even here we underestimate the emotional part of the mind at our peril, because if people do not have their heart in doing something they may not do it very well. The part of our mind that makes judgments and tries to exercise control drives most of what we do at work but there is a fine balance between the demands of a selfish and manipulative ego and the humble awareness of larger-than-self goals that will benefit everyone involved.

Shared meaning is not always a pleasant experience. What you perceive about another person comes partly from him or her and partly from your own mind. I know that if someone criticises me and I already feel inadequate in that respect the shared meaning is especially unpleasant. If I can separate my own opinion from that expressed by the other person the only shared meaning might be that we agree to disagree. I learned that my lack of confidence in myself was an obstacle to obtaining shared meaning. If we haven't connected with others from a place that feels worthy we are more sensitive to criticism and so we may feel the need to either argue the point to put them down or keep trying to please them. Inappropriate people-pleasing was a feature of my dark times.

Our self-esteem, by equipping us to be comfortable with our own feelings, also makes possible the wonderful human connections that we call **empathy** and **compassion**. Empathy is a special form of shared meaning in which both parties feel they can understand what the other is feeling. It begins with being non-judgmental, which makes it different from sympathy where we tend to separate ourselves from others by judging them. You don't have to feel exactly the same feelings to empathise with someone but you do have to open your mind and imagine you can listen with your heart. This shared meaning might even be subconscious such as when a grandparent empathises with her grandchild who is coming of age about feelings that are strange and new to the youngster, but understood only too well by the older person. This sharing occurs beneath and beyond conscious thought.

The idea from research in monkeys that there are 'mirror neurons' in our brain that respond directly to tiny clues we pick up about another person's actions or intentions has excited many researchers in recent decades. It sounds like a good explanation for our empathic ability and there may be a 'mirror neuron system' in humans in which the 'spindle cells' may be involved but this has not yet been properly substantiated in our species. It will probably turn out to play a part. It is also an example of the way we are attracted to simple mechanistic explanations for processes of the mind that are so complex they may never be completely understood. The famous fictional character, Harry Potter, was chastised by Professor Snape for thinking that the villain, Voldemort, could extract feelings and memories from another person's mind by 'mind-reading.' Snape showed his knowledge of neuroscience when he said, 'you have no subtlety, Potter. Only Muggles talk of mind-reading. The mind is not a book.'

Barack Obama called for Americans to address the 'empathy deficit' in their society – an unusual request in the political context where a deficit usually refers to finances. An American futurist, Jeremy Rifkin, wrote passionately in his book, *The Empathic Civilization*, that empathy has been appreciated and understood only fairly recently in our social evolution and will be needed to cope with our looming environmental and ecological crises. He says there is a 'dawning realisation that we are a fundamentally empathic species' and that this level of shared meaning on a global scale is our best hope for the survival of our species.

Compassion is one of our greatest gifts and most worthwhile endeavours, as the Tibetan Dalai Lama reminds us quite often. Our opportunity to witness human suffering on a large scale has never been greater with, for example, the refugee crises across the world and ongoing wars. Like empathy, compassion requires us to see the other person as fundamentally not different from ourselves yet the shared meaning includes a recognition of that person's special needs and desire for those needs to be met. An unselfish, benevolent concern for the good of another person is an acknowledgment that we all suffer and also that we believe in the relief of suffering as our universal human right. We still must trust in the unknown because compassion will burn out if it is too tightly tied to specific outcomes.

Compassionate friends are the most likely relievers of our suffering but the therapist-patient relationship has become increasingly important. No matter what type of therapy it is there will be shared meaning involved. Pilar Jennings, an experienced Buddhist psychoanalyst, writes about this in her book, *Mixing Minds – The Power of Relationship in Psychotherapy and Buddhism*. She says 'we cannot find ourselves or be ourselves alone' so doctor-patient inequalities and diagnostic details are not helpful if they obscure the compassionate relationship. My favourite author-psychotherapist, Irving Yalom, says that he often reminds himself: 'it's the relationship that heals, the relationship that heals . . .'

Compassion applied to oneself is an important and subtle kind of shared meaning that I did not understand when I spent a lot of time in rumination and self-pity. The default zone of our brain can often be employed in negative judgment, dwelling on past mistakes and criticisms that have hurt our feelings. Real compassion does not consist of judgment or criticism –

it is an expression of love. Self-forgiveness is an awareness of our inherent imperfection and vulnerability, revealed by our emotions, followed by an acceptance that this is perfectly okay.

Perhaps the biggest mystery of the mind is that we could share meaning with something outside of ourselves that is unknown. John O'Donohue refers to our soul as a 'divine echo that whispers in every heart' in his book, *Eternal Echoes*, about our yearning to belong. 'The shelter of belonging empowers you,' he says, but it also never extinguishes the flame of further longing and the desire to connect. My relationship with the unknown feels more like an opening of space in my mind than a direct quest for shared meaning.

A fundamental characteristic of yearning is our deeply felt need for movement – our sense of rhythm and cadence and flow. Our evolution has included singing and dancing, possibly for hundreds of thousands of years, so a subtle sense is built into us which surely enables us to sense the inner movement in others. When we experience empathy and compassion we feel we are moving together – on the same wavelength – as if we are a partners on a dance floor or singing a duet.

What we have in common with all living things is that we seek to connect in a meaningful way. Biophilia – literally love of life – is an instinctive bond between all living things. The term was first introduced by Erich Fromm and developed into a serious hypothesis by E. O. Wilson in his book, *Biophilia*, over 30 years ago. Our search for a common thread that explains aliveness is perhaps the most fundamental shared meaning and it is also our link with the natural world.

## Chapter 12

## Everyday Love

A grand philosophical vision of love would be of little use if we could not practice love in our everyday lives. I began this story with a mother and new baby. If we become parents we immediately find that our attention is drawn towards practical loving care. Every single one of us will be touched by love in some way and it will be the strongest sense of bonding we will ever know. It will also be the source of our greatest pain.

My friend Rachael had a habit of falling in love with a new man every few months in her early years and the highs and lows she went through were her way of seeking external cures for her own bad feelings. She neglected the inner resources of her mind in the same way I did until she reached her thirties, but unlike me she always had a busy social life. Our fundamental frustration was the same – a yearning for love – and neither of us found any satisfaction until we began to do some things differently. With too much self-consciousness occupying our minds our ability to love was restricted, which is probably why we both appreciate it so much in our lives today.

I've already mentioned Erich Fromm's book, *The Art of Loving*, which has remained in print for 60 years carrying the important message that we have to learn the art of love by practicing it every day. Several misconceptions are common: firstly that we simply 'fall' into it so there is nothing to do and secondly, that this happens so easily we can assume it will last forever automatically. We also tend to think more about being loved than giving it to others. The result is that we take the whole idea of love for granted and forget to put effort into it on a regular basis. Just as being is doing so love is all about doing – a verb as well as a noun.

This is seen first in the attention a new mother gives to her child who has come into the world with an obvious expectation of being loved. The words and actions are rudimentary at first yet the feelings of connectedness are sufficient for both parties to learn what it means to express love and to feel that you are loved. We also learn the important practical lesson that love does not rid your life of all problems.

Parental love is the primary tool for teaching and learning about not getting your needs met all the time and being able to move between secure attachment and comfortable separation as required. This is crucial for learning that the feelings of inadequacy and neediness that arise in our emotions do not actually mean that we are not lovable or not loved. Love is not just one of our emotions; it is something beyond them that will always support our aliveness if we exercise it. I had to learn that it's okay to be imperfect and to make mistakes and that this does not deny us the experience of love – in fact it shows us how it works.

Fear is a primary emotion that interacts with love all the time and although that tension is a necessary part of our aliveness, too much fear can block our ability to love if we don't have enough trust and faith in the unknown. The very idea of love is to relinquish the need to control and judge and accept being here and now in whatever circumstances we find ourselves. There is never a time when we cannot decide to offer something outwards from ourselves towards others in the name of love. Then, in defiance of logic, the more of it you give away the more there seems to be in your own life. Giving is not the same as giving up something; in fact it's an indication that you have enough to spare. 'It is not he who has much who is rich, but he who gives much' as Fromm put it.

I've mentioned three different levels at which loving relationships can be formed. As well as the relationship with another person there is the relationship with oneself and, thirdly, with the unknown. To understand this as a hierarchy is a practical boon that I use a lot. When we strike relationship problems we often put all our effort into the lowest level, trying to sort it out with another person, but the problem also stems from a felt lack of love at one or both of the higher levels. I felt I had no love in my life during those dark times and my recovery from this could not be negotiated solely with other people. I only learned to love others as I learned to love myself in a healthy way and this happened when I had developed a better relationship with the unknown.

The practice of love is not always going to be smooth sailing of course. The intimacy and connection provided by love still honours all the differences between two people – they are still there to prickle and cause stress. Each of us has an autonomous *will* that does not necessarily align with the needs of others or with the common good. Rollo May emphasises the interdependence of these two great forces in his book *Love and Will*. He says that without love our will simply ends up as manipulation but by the same token, love without any will would be rather empty and diffuse.

We obtain the confidence to love others from being comfortable with ourselves, feeling that we are already well enough endowed to give love away. Rollo May also points out that there is no contradiction between love of others and the love of yourself and selfishness stems more often from a lack of self-love. If the stories we create diminish our self-worth they weaken our natural ability to love.

The noise that Tolle talks about that is generated by the egoic self is the problem. An egoic kind of relationship is driven by selfish wanting, which includes the ego's favourite tools of criticising and complaining, or by the only real alternative it knows, which is indifference. Even hatred, which is a passion, is not so much an enemy of love as indifference. It is the state of mind that most thoroughly denigrates and denies the vitality of our mind.

There is no better reminder of one's vitality than the feeling of falling in love. It is a magical combination of lightness and strength whereby your physiology seems to be optimised so that your heart actually sings, your spirits soar and a smile seems to have been planted on your face. There is no better example of the upside of stress than the time you spend exploring interesting congruencies and differences with a new lover. It is exciting and stressful, which carries the energy of aliveness.

Most people writing about love emphasise the positive effects that go with social engagement including the pleasure of shared meaning, the bonding influence of oxytocin and the warm glow we get from the soothing ANS. Barbara Fredrickson in her book *Love 2.0* calls each experience of love a moment of 'positivity resonance' and she adds to this the idea that an accumulation of positive emotions is the best way to 'broaden-and-build' our minds and our lives. Her idea of this as a new 'version' of love is that these moments of resonance occur all the time, even between strangers, rather than being confined to a particular relationship. It depends where we are putting our attention and the challenge is to maintain our awareness of spontaneous exchanges even in long-term relationships.

The trouble with romantic love is that it doesn't become a long-lasting asset for us unless it extends more deeply into the depths of our mind that include our soul. Love is such a fundamental aspect of life that its experience at a superficial level can never do it justice. Eckhart Tolle points out in *A New Earth* that the heights of romance are intensifications of just the kind of reactive exchanges that our ego delights in so they will not satisfy us at a deeper level or for a long time.

The noted Jungian author, Robert Johnson, in a book called *We: Understanding the Psychology of Romantic Love*, uses the mythical story of *Tristan and Iseult* to explain that romantic love teaches us an important lesson through its superficiality. Tristan's mother died on the day he was born and he grew up in a man's world. When he fell in love with Iseult they drank a love potion that turned their world into a beautiful fantasy. He was never able to convert this energy into a deeper spiritual connection because he tried to possess her with his egoic self. It is a complex and ultimately tragic story immortalised by Wagner's opera with its particular form of discord known as the 'Tristan chord' that has been called the most splendid expression of unrequited love. Johnson says that Tristan did not 'heed his soul' and in the end it 'snares him through his selfish pride.'

The altered states of consciousness that may occur in the trance of love are often demeaned as unrealistic – the false impressions of a star-crossed or intoxicated imagination – and this is true so far as the egoic self is concerned. Severe pain results from losing touch with reality; the fantasy world such as Tristan lived in comes crashing down eventually and the resulting loss and loneliness is our most intense kind of grief. The reactivity of the egoic self makes love a more likely cause of violent arguments than any other subject. In this case the differences between us take precedence over the common bond of our aliveness.

By acknowledging love we are saying that the connectedness is stronger than the differences that are creating the tension. Doing this also opens an avenue for connecting with people whom you feel are your enemies or whom you dislike or avoid because they have criticised and annoyed you. Weighed down by ego your mind sees only their faults, but buoyed by love it is possible to see that they also have good in them. Acts of forgiveness and the ancient idea of praying for your enemies are actually the most reliable ways of undoing one's troublesome ego. I conclude from this that there is something in our souls that wants us to bring the good to the fore. Trying to bring out the best in others is the simplest and most successful way of bringing out the best in yourself.

This is exemplified in the power of the smile – perhaps the simplest and truest manifestation of everyday love. There is extensive research showing that every aspect of interpersonal life is enhanced by the behaviour of smiling, whether it is in conducting business, coping with stress, relieving suffering or just having fun. When you smile you feel better and you bring out the good in others as well as yourself. On the other hand, the loss of a long-lasting love is the deepest possible sadness and we experience grief as one of our primary, instinctual emotions that needs to be honoured and endured.

The everyday experience of love is not generally a state of bliss but it is the most deeply meaningful and satisfying experience of all. I re-married in my mid-forties and one of the passages from Robert Johnson's book, *We*, that my wife, Penelope, and I enjoyed reading together was about a 'stirring the oatmeal' kind of love, which is what I am calling everyday love. It is in doing chores together or simply walking around the garden or sitting together in the evening that I think many couples find that love is indeed 'the proper use of the mind.' It's as subtle as eye contact, a tilt of the head, a slight touch or a warm smile. It is a connection through physical as well as mental activity, playing and laughing together, and of course sexual intercourse or making love, which can be the supreme physiological bond between two people.

Mutual respect is implied in my earlier claim that, at a deeper level, we legitimise what we love and therefore only see things as they really are when we look at them with love, without judgment or the desire to control or the wish for them to be anything other than what they are. 'It is only with the heart that one can see rightly; what is essential is invisible to the eye' says Antoine Saint-Exupery in *The Little Prince*. Love is also described by Robert Johnson as 'the power within us that affirms and values another human being as he or she is . . . at its very essence it is an appreciation – a recognition of value.' We will consider values in more detail shortly.

I have come to believe it is my biological birthright to know that I am loved and that this makes it possible for me to engage with the world from a position of worthiness much of the time. On a day when, to my chagrin, that is not happening I have learned to address my relationship with the unknown in the first instance and thus be a little kinder towards myself. Even a glimmer of renewed hope resulting from that helps me to connect and share meaningfully with other people once again. This is the simple idea of everyday love that I have found to be more powerful than any of the destructive forces I have encountered in my life so far.

Because love is a doing, you have to notice it to receive it and be aware of it to offer it to others. Whether we notice it or not and whether we express it depends on where we choose to direct our attention.

# Chapter 13

# Attention and Awareness

'Tell me what you pay attention to and I will tell you who you are.' So said the Spanish philosopher, José Ortega y Gasset, a hundred years ago. The fact that our mind controls our attention and is controlled by our attention makes his statement even more pertinent to the science of mind today.

Attention is not just another thing the mind does – it sets the stage for everything because our mind can only work with the connections it has made and these are selected from a much larger range of possibilities. Making connections is what our mind does and making connections is *attending*. What we perceive the world to be depends on where we direct our attention and then what we have found influences what we will look for next. We fail to notice what we have failed to notice so there are always blind spots that may come to light when there is a crisis.

This means that the world as we know it has been shaped by our awareness of it and we ourselves are being shaped in that process. We became ourselves as a result of all that has happened in our relationships with one another and with the rest of the world. Our autonomy and our connectedness are inextricably bound and the way we connect is the nub of what we call free will – we can choose where to direct our attention.

This is important not just because you and I might notice different things. The real issue is that our mind needs two different kinds of attention process. It needs a concentrated attention to discern the details and it needs a broader awareness to understand the context and thereby create a satisfying meaning. I referred to this earlier with a quote from Owen Barfield that knowing more and more about how things work we find less and less meaning in them. We need to know cause and effect and mechanistic relations for our mind to utilise and manipulate what it connects with, but we need to know quite different qualities such as context and wholeness, which includes the unknown, for our mind to make satisfying meaning. These two processes are not mutually exclusive but when we favour attention to detail we inevitably lose some of our context awareness and vice versa.

The most intriguing mystery in mind science for hundreds of years has been why we have two sides of our brain – two distinct hemispheres that are connected by a central trunk of nerves but yet have different connectivity patterns that manifest differently in our experience. The brain structures are all duplicated, but not symmetrically; the right side is larger and heavier and differs in cell structure and shape. Brain damage has quite different effects depending on which side it is on. Simplistic explanations about this swept into popular psychology after split-brain experiments in the 1960's showed more language abilities in the left hemisphere and more spatio-visual abilities on the right. Subsequent research led the scientific community to reject this idea because there is activity all over the brain whether we are speaking or drawing or doing anything else. Although a distinct laterality is evident in every animal that has a brain, the quest to understand why this is so seemed to die in its tracks. I think this was partly due to scientific hubris on the part of brain researchers; I know that some scientists resent popular interpretations that are a gross oversimplification of subjects they rightly see as complex.

When I was researching stress I was attached for a time to a Neuroscience and Behaviour Group led by Professor Lesley Rogers who was a world authority on brain laterality in birds and animals. Most of the nerves to and from the left side of our body go to the right side of our brain and vice versa. The way that birds and some animals see things is simpler than humans in that each eye is entirely controlled by the opposite side of the brain. Therefore Lesley Rogers and others were able to show, for example, that birds use their left brain for attending to fine detail such as pecking and picking up seeds and their right brain for keeping in touch with others of their kind, watching for predators and surveying the world in general. There is a clue in this about the human brain.

Another clue comes from studies of the nerve trunk (the corpus callosum) that connects the two hemispheres in the human brain. Networks of nerves can either speed up or slow down their process under the influence of different neurotransmitters that are either stimulatory or inhibitory. It turns out that the corpus callosum is largely inhibitory in its function, even though it also allows a communication flow, which suggests that the two hemispheres combine by resisting and steadying one another to achieve the best result; they have different, but complementary roles. A surgeon and his assistant can't be making the same incision – they need to do different things to work together effectively. Another example that is called 'opponent processing' is when you use one hand to steady the other to make a very careful movement.

It was a British researcher, Iain McGilchrist, whose academic background was originally in the arts, then in brain neuroimaging and thirdly as an eminent psychiatrist in London, who dared to reopen the question about brain laterality and his studies are the most thorough ever undertaken. They are described in his book *The Master and His Emissary – The Divided Brain and the Making of the Western World*. As its title suggests this monumental work outlines the cultural significance of the way we use our brains. He poses a related question in shorter e-book called *The Divided Brain and the Search for Meaning – Why Are We So Unhappy?*

McGilchrist's idea is that the two different and complementary kinds of attention process that we need are made possible by the division of our brain into two functional units. When our priority is to attend to cause-effect manipulation we will favour left-brain operations and while our priority is to appreciate context and broader relationships to obtain awareness and meaning we will direct our attention in such a way that we favour the activity of our right hemisphere. Our left-brain processes are ideally suited for logical attention to detail and purposeful manipulation to achieve results while our right-brain processes are needed to apprehend other qualities of our mind that are less precise, but absolutely essential for the feeling of meaning.

Our feelings and emotions and our interpersonal connections depend much more on the right hemisphere than the left. All the feelings around social engagement (except anger) show up mostly on the right side when the brain is scanned and the new soothing ANS is lateralised on the right. Crucially, the ability to learn something new, to be creative, to understand metaphor and appreciate music, beauty and value that includes the unknown requires the deliberate involvement of our right hemisphere.

One would assume that the meaning-generator is the natural leader in the proper use of our mind and the detail-manager is its very valuable subordinate, but McGilchrist is saying that our minds have a problem today because the subordinate has been gradually taking over. His book title, *The Master and his Emissary*, is taken from a story told by Nietzsche about an emissary to whom the master had delegated tasks who then extended these responsibilities to eventually control the whole kingdom. That we have become 'left-shifted' in this way is now a fairly common phrase in popular mind science. McGilchrist's subtitle regarding *the Making of the Western World* refers to the way that Western culture has gradually become shallower and more mechanistic and we are losing some of our sensitivity, spirituality and ability to find meaning as we favour our left brain more and more at the expense of the right.

These two ways of paying attention are sufficiently different that they can generate two different realities if they are not integrated continually. We can become highly attentive without being highly aware. The left brain is very good at utilising what it already knows, where precision and logical procedures are required, but it is not open to what is novel or uncertain. Its blind spot is being thoroughly self-satisfied, convinced by its own internal consistency – a state of mind that appeals to our egoic self. It builds a world that is more and more like itself and flatters itself with this knowledge, not realising that it lives in a hall of mirrors where the exits are concealed (to use McGilchrist's apt metaphor). If we can't see what we do not think is there our mind is led towards the illusion of certainty and away from being able to say that perhaps we don't know, which is the humility that comes with a broader awareness.

The right-brain process or mode of attention enables us to recognise non-literal relationships such as metaphor and analogy, to generate feelings, to appreciate art and music and to understand the nuances of social engagement. It is sensitive to what is new or mysterious so it's essential for learning. The satisfaction it brings us is not the narrow selfish kind of knowing. It is the sense of belonging to something bigger than ourselves, which provides a deeper kind of meaning. Whereas the left brain objectifies people and situations, it is the right that facilitates empathy, compassion and authentic social engagement. Excessive judging and trying to control are modes of attention in which the right brain is neglected.

Being a scientist I needed to abstract and generalise. My mind had to organise things and it is a feature of left-brain attention that we can aggregate and sort the bits into categories to create the artificial sense of order that we like so much for our work. But this comes at a cost. Over time the categories become so real to us that we end up, against our better instincts, pigeonholing things and idly ticking boxes rather than examining the items themselves. This is not reality, but a representation of reality that we have created that can end up seeming to be real such as when something written on a piece of paper is regarded more highly than the actual situation that people are experiencing. The right-brain mode of attention provides an awareness that is more accurate and prioritises people ahead of the systems. The objectification is better suited to controlling than to caring. I often think of the poignant words of E. F. Schumacher in *A Guide for the Perplexed* where he suggests that we should design systems 'as if people mattered.'

Also as a scientist I was keen on defining and naming things precisely. This can be very useful but it also puts limitations on the meanings we can form. John O'Donohue speaks in *Eternal Echoes* about the way the mind's fixity robs us of the freedom that our imagination needs to play its role. He said we 'bind our lives in chains of forced connections' with too much rigidity and that 'certainty freezes the mind.' What is nameless is important because it allows one's meanings to grow and develop in the natural course of events. 'The business of the soul cannot be framed' as O'Donohue puts it.

Flow rather than fixity is the difference between animate and inanimate – the sure sign of aliveness. Explicitness is needed in much of what we do but it also narrows our imagination. There is a world of difference between the hand that grasps and pins meaning down and the hand that reaches out in openness and love. We need both.

Mainstream neuroscientists have not rushed to agree with McGilchrist's explanation. Michael Gazzaniga, for example, refers to the left hemisphere as 'dominant' and calls it 'the interpreter' whereas he sees the right hemisphere's involvement in our experience of the arts and humanities as an added extra that we could easily do without. Steven Pinker is another who is disdainful about the importance of the humanities for our mind. Stephen Kosslyn and Wayne Miller, in their book *Top Brain, Bottom Brain*, dismiss laterality in favour of the idea that the lower brain receives the information and our higher reasoning decides what to do with it. One wonders if these are left-shifted perspectives.

The prevailing framework of rationalism affects everything we do and our culture is highly systematised by bureaucratic rules and regulations. Feelings of satisfaction are harder to find in this culture and feelings of dissatisfaction are all too common. It is an unintended, yet serious, loss of sensitivity and a deterioration of the feeling function of our mind. The ecological difficulties we face won't be solved without creativity and sensitivity. It feels uncomfortable to admit this if you are looking for easy solutions. We often shift to the left to try to avoid emotional pain and discomfort but the left can't let go and trust the bigger picture so we do not get the relief that comes from accepting and owning our feelings.

There are quite a few mind scientists in America who have embraced ideas from Buddhist practice; Francisco Varela whom I mentioned earlier was a leader in this respect. Researchers such as Richie Davidson who wrote *The Emotional Life of Your Brain* (with Sharon Begley) have shown that mindfulness meditation affects brain activity quite profoundly because it improves connectivity and integration. Focussed attention on your breath as it flows is the most powerful way of connecting your conscious mind with the ANS self-regulation of heartrate and breathing. Steadying the mind has many benefits but I question their idea that strengthening concentration and control, which shows up in the left prefrontal cortex and has been labelled 'happiness', is necessarily a good thing if it is at the expense of the sadness and compassion that shows up in the right prefrontal cortex. We need sadness as well to know softness – too much hardness can break things.

Being able to hold your train of attention is an important mental attribute and there is much concern today about 'attention deficit disorders' particularly amongst younger people. Mindfulness practice will be helpful in this regard. The best definition I've seen of effective meditation is 'to optimise the interaction between attention and awareness.' It comes from John Yates, a Buddhist neuroscientist who wrote *The Mind Illuminated*, who suggests that we actually have an *'awareness* deficit disorder' in our society today. Ideally our attention informs our awareness and vice versa so if either is haphazard the other is affected.

There is a cultural revolution occurring in our attention style that is such a big subject I can't deal with it here except as an aside. The small screen on a smartphone, tablet or computer has hijacked our attention more dramatically than any other new technology in our history. The change has happened so quickly it's hard to believe that many people in a modern society spend more of their day looking at a silver screen than doing anything else. Our social engagement will be different when we channel it through an intermediary device. In a book called *The World Beyond Your Head* Matthew Crawford points out that our connectedness is now shaped and regulated by the engineers who design the systems of social media and electronic commerce. Because our culture arises from our conversation this is changing our world.

I see no point in being pessimistic because our minds are marvels of adaptation, especially when we are young. We do have a responsibility, however, to safeguard the biological necessities of maintaining autonomy and connecting wisely even as we extend the reach and the convenience of our connectedness through artificial means. I share with Sherry Turkle who wrote *Alone Together* and more recently *Reclaiming Conversation*, at least some of her concern that so many young people prefer the asynchronous, text-based, 'disembodied' mode of conversation ahead of actually speaking to someone (even on the phone), apparently because they find it 'less demanding emotionally' and 'more efficient.' It's true that the emotional part of the connection is the most demanding and the least efficient part, but to try to distance yourself from it, which the IT barons call 'reducing friction,' will be a challenge for the health of our minds.

Someone said that inveterate texters might be 'all thumbs' when it comes to face-to-face relations! They will find ways to connect nevertheless.

Our ever-expanding reliance on automation has brought many changes over the years in the way we use our minds, especially our attention. It was designed to make our lives easier – less burdensome – as it also improved productivity. In doing this it has made the mind's connection with the natural world less secure in some quite alarming ways. In a book called *The Glass Cage* Nicholas Carr explains how the use of autopilots has actually de-skilled pilots, professional people from architects to doctors don't bother to make decisions that an 'expert system' has already made for them and satellite navigation systems have eroded our personal sense of where we are – to mention only a few. My doctor spends less time looking at me when I visit him now because he needs to spend more time looking at his computer. Technology gets between us and our world in a way that weakens our connectedness because we don't have our hands on the things themselves and we lose skills that are not being used. In another book, *The Shallows*, Carr explains how the internet is changing the way we think, read and remember things.

Since the very first tool-making experience, technology has brought us benefits, the trade-off being that it drives the evolution of our mind. The rate of its development easily outstrips our biological capability to evolve. Thus we need the power of humanness that is our experience of love more than ever. Technology has often given us what we don't need at the expense of what we do. This distinction between wants and needs will always be difficult for us to handle. It is paralleled in our minds by the difference between self and soul.

## Chapter 14

## Too Much Self

The aphorism 'know thyself' has an interesting history, which adds to its mystique, yet it has always been a statement about humility in relation to gods of some kind. It is said to have originated in Ancient Egypt, though it is more commonly associated with Pythia, the priestess and oracle at Delphi in Ancient Greece where the words were inscribed on the forecourt of the Temple of Solomon. Pythia was reputed to give long-winded, ambiguous answers to any question as oracles are wont to do. Even so, 'know thyself' and 'nothing in excess' became catchphrases in popular culture. Plato and most other philosophers used them extensively and people still write theses on them today without necessarily clarifying the relationship between self and something greater than self.

Undoubtedly my own experience of self-pity and self-condemnation did more harm than good for the use of my mind. We need our autonomy yet, paradoxically, the 'self' is also the last thing we need to spend time thinking, talking or worrying about. A wise friend told me once that 'know yourself' is only useful when it is followed by 'accept yourself' and then 'forget yourself.' That makes it clearly a statement about humility. I said earlier that the smaller my sense of self in relation to everything else the larger my sense of belonging seems to be.

Yet we do need a sense of self and the default zone in our brain works hard at this. We need an identity to create the story of our relationships with other people and interactions with the world. When people are in solitary confinement for long periods they tend to lose their mind and may not know who they are. A defence against this is supposed to be speaking as in conversation with imaginary friends and people that you have known, which keeps alive your sense of who you are. I think the lesson from this is that we create our sense of self from our interactions with other people so we don't need to try too hard to do it on our own.

The introspection going on in our brain is part of the larger aspect of our mind that I have been calling our *imagination*. I have lauded this and said we cannot do without it. At the same time it was the source of my greatest pain and suffering in those early years. Imagination seems real to the brain but it is not reality and when one lives too much in fantasy and gets out of touch with reality as I did there can be no satisfaction. The everyday use of our mind depends on where we direct our attention and what we are *doing* at each moment. If we fail to attend to our relationships because too much of our mind is self-directed we sabotage our ability to engage, to love, and to be happy.

The Sydney psychiatrist I mentioned in Chapter 3, Julian Short, said the two ways of being and doing that help us most are **kindness** (for our relationships) and ***dignity*** (for our autonomy.) Dignity is a lovely word to describe being confident in yourself in a humble rather than a prideful way. Self-esteem is actually not judging yourself in a positive way – it is relating to yourself kindly. Self-confidence is entirely different from pride. It comes not from celebrating past achievements or expecting future ones; it comes from being in the present moment with a feeling of faith and trust. We often feel that we're living in a rut and don't have much free will because we are controlled by whatever happened beforehand or what could happen next. The present moment is the only time that all possibilities are truly open to us yet our mind spends a lot of time elsewhere. In the practice of mindfulness we draw confidence in the present moment from the feeling of trust in a life process that is bigger than oneself.

Lacking this perspective we experience a false pride rather than the one that manifests as feeling worthy. Pride heads the list of a well-known catalogue of human imperfections known as the Seven Deadly Sins. I learned from Ernest Kurtz and Katherine Ketcham in their book *The Spirituality of Imperfection* that Evagrius Ponticus (an Egyptian monk in the 4$^{th}$ century AD) originally formulated this list of what he called 'bad habits' that he thought were the causes of our emotional problems. Religions make much of the word 'sin' even though its derivation is from a word meaning 'missing the target' that can be interpreted as living unskilfully;

Evagrius thought these were the everyday faults of the mind that were the most common 'enemies of the soul.' Gluttony was his own downfall, apparently, to which he added anger, avarice, envy, fornication (now called lust) and acedia (now called sloth). He had two more that are now combined into one called pride. All of them are self-serving and self-centred; not one of them is humble. Selfish pride is the improper use of mind that bedevilled my life most severely because I did not realise that it is the dancing-partner of the insidious emotion of shame.

Eckhart Tolle wrote about the problems caused by too much self in his book *A New Earth*. The egoic self likes to play roles such as 'victim' or 'villain' as well as those of self-aggrandisement. False pride is equally suited to being bad as being good; in fact this is its more common manifestation. In love there is no sense of superior or inferior. Many of us have used our roles in the workplace as a kind of escape because they enable us to be someone a little different from the version of ourselves that might be having difficulties elsewhere. Happiness is a role that people like to play at times – and unhappiness too. Discussing things as an adult with your parents (or with ex-partners) is always difficult because, despite your best intentions to avoid this, you are likely to slip into your role from the past with all the subconscious history that entails.

Your thoughts and the voice in your head are not who you are. When you see that you are not what they are telling you there is a better chance that the real you can express itself. Tolle recommends being comfortable with not knowing who you are because you will be who you are anyway! The self that you will come to love will be the self that you really are. If you feel you need a certain sense of 'self' to protect you, that will not work. Defining yourself through thought is limiting to yourself and to your relationships in the same way that all superficial thinking narrows our existence. John O'Donohue calls this the 'cage of frightened identity' and he says that we often fall back on the 'refuge of false belonging.'

One of the worst lies our mind can tell us is that we are unworthy. Rollo May pointed out that we use self-condemnation is an arrogant substitute for self-worth. Being unworthy and being imperfect are very different. Everyone is imperfect and, as I said, our strength arises from recognising our vulnerability and not trying to hide it from others. Perfectionism is an inhuman aim activated by trying to please everybody, including yourself, all the time. Dignity includes not seeing yourself as being whatever other people say about you. Your ego takes everything personally, but other people's perceptions are primarily the result of their experience and their story and often have little to do with you anyway.

The everyday feelings of inadequacy that, nevertheless, seem to be so common for all of us show up in an extraordinary amount of hero worship whereby sports stars, entertainers and TV celebrities become a kind of *alter ego*. Feeling unworthy also affects our attitude to scarcity, which is the feeling that you never have quite enough. The ego thrives on wanting rather than having so it couldn't ever be satisfied anyway and the opposite of scarcity doesn't have to be abundance; it could simply be enough, as Brené Brown likes to say.

I said earlier that we tend to make more judgments than are really necessary and from these we form opinions that our egoic self would like others to hear. Social media such as Twitter and Facebook have expanded our opportunities in this regard. I do this too, but over time I came to the conclusion that, although I need to make some judgments to help me act appropriately, I am surely not in this world to be the judge of everything that happens. There can be a nice easing of tension in your mind when you are not clinging to your opinions and you can allow them to change. Whenever we put up resistance, which we need to do at times, we will notice that whatever we are resisting will push back accordingly and will persist in our mind. We can always remove the power we have given it by choosing not to resist at this point in time.

The egoic self is more active in our everyday mind than the true self. Ego is a form of boundary protection so it's basically not in favour of connectedness and likes to play what John O'Donohue calls a 'false game of judgment, comparison and assumption.' Unhealthy rumination, unnecessary judgments and thinking about control are the opposite of authentic mindfulness; the best way to put these gremlins of our selfish ego out of business is by having faith in the present moment.

Prometheus was a Titan in Greek mythology who stole fire from the gods and gave it to humans to use as the creative force of knowledge. For this deed he suffered a terrible punishment in which he was tied to a rock where an eagle came and ate his liver every day. The modern day Frankenstein who created life in an unnatural way for his own purposes is one of many offshoots from this ancient story, which seems to me to be a reminder that what we believe we know can be very useful in the service of our relationships, but it can be a dangerous master if we take it too seriously and use it selfishly.

Undue regard for the self is a neglect of the soul, which is where the love comes from – for me. But your smile is an act of love so if you can smile at your own ego you are much less likely to be ruled by it.

# Chapter 15

# Suffering

That we suffer is not only the Buddhist's first Noble Truth – it's a fact well known to us all. What we expect of our mind is to help us keep it to a minimum. This can be tricky because the way we use our mind can also be a cause of our suffering. There is much that is mysterious about pain and suffering. We are advised to think of them as separate, the suffering being a secondary reaction to the pain, and some can do this better than others. The extraordinary endurance and resilience of some people in the face of pain is another of the natural wonders of the mind. At the other extreme are people who are so sensitive that complaining is their default mindset. The egoic self enjoys this because complaining, blaming and resenting are its favourite tools for shoring up its own position. The ego would generally prefer to be right than to be at peace.

Because our need for social engagement is so great there is much suffering due to loneliness and this appears to be a worsening problem. According to John Cacciopo and William Patrick in their book, *Loneliness – Human Nature and the Need for Social Connection*, 20% of Americans now feel sufficiently disconnected for it to be affecting their health. They found that loneliness was on a par with obesity, high blood pressure, lack of exercise and smoking as a risk factor for illness or early death. They showed that it is not just any form of social support that will overcome loneliness – there has to be genuine shared meaning in the connection.

It's hard to describe suffering adequately because, like happiness, it is an amalgam of emotions, feelings and thoughts – a very complex state of mind. The way we direct our attention is crucial and we seem to lose control over this at times. In a book called *Capture – Unravelling the Mystery of Mental Suffering* David Kessler writes about the way that certain things capture our attention so powerfully we cannot seem to turn it elsewhere even though we want to do that. These obsessions contribute to suffering in two ways: they prevent us from being truly present with whatever is happening now and they concentrate too much of our mind's activity on the self rather than the soul. As he says, there is no switch to turn off this capture so we need to draw strength from outside of ourselves by building broader connections, even though that will be difficult to do.

What I think is important about his work is that he sees a common mechanism for many different forms of suffering. He says that doctors often try to heal suffering by treating a very specific underlying cause such as a certain chemical imbalance whereas there may be a more general problem that is not addressed by this treatment and the treatment may even compound the problem. PTSD, for example, is an inability to be alive in the present situation because the mind's attention has been hijacked by the past trauma and there is insufficient awareness to recognise this. Some medications dampen awareness even more.

If we forget the basic principle that our mind's purpose is to promote being and belonging we open the door to the unfortunate habits that I mentioned first in Chapter 4 – unnecessary judgment and the desire to control. It is the nature of our mind to try to predict the future and then the craving for certainty fuels our desire to control, which is probably our biggest curse. Feeling that you don't have control over your life predisposes to anxiety and depression whereas feeling that you don't *need* to have control over everything is liberating. This need to control is set in the parts of our mind that create the most noise and tell us the biggest lies and wherever there is control or the desire to control, love will be harder to find.

Interactions involving our egoic self are conspicuous in their reactivity, which we often call 'drama.' Love, empathy and compassion work because they don't fuel the drama or buy into the reactivity. We begin life with a set of primary emotions and onto these we build our everyday emotional repertoire as a result of this reactivity that we experience in our dealings with others, especially as children, but throughout our whole lives. It is often the case that a parent's emotional reactivity shows up in a child's later life. Guilt and shame, jealousy, envy and resentment, gluttony, selfish lust, sloth, contempt, cynicism and indifference all carry the painful feelings of suffering. Sadness, anxiety and depression are more complex and mysterious variations.

Martha Nussbaum points out in her book *Upheavals of Thought – The Intelligence of Emotions* that the purpose of emotions is to reveal our inadequacies, to highlight our limitations and vulnerability, so we may have a more honest appreciation of the reality of our lives. They help us to acknowledge our neediness and lack of self-sufficiency – to realise that in reality there is much we can't control.

She says this neediness is shrouded in our shame because we don't want to acknowledge it. We are probably the only animals who wish not to be emotional; we would like to transcend them, but know we can't. Thus we are the only animals for whom neediness is a source of shame and so we adopt a false pride to deny that we are needy. In growing up we have to learn through discomfort and frustration that neediness is okay – in fact, it is essential for the growth and development of our mind. Permitting ourselves to be needy is part of our emerging understanding of love and the letting go of our demand for perfection. The child's feelings are a mix of omnipotence and helplessness and he or she learns to move from one to the other as required. *To remain intolerant towards imperfection as we grow up is a serious handicap.* The dominant emotion under the tyranny of perfectionism is a false pride that is accompanied by shame.

I think that shame is the most subtle and the most prevalent of the subconscious emotions of suffering because it is the one that prevents us from knowing that we are loved. Guilt and shame may occur together. The guilt is easier to deal with because it results from something you know you have done wrong and therefore you can at least apologise and perhaps make restitution. Shame is a self-judgment that you are not worthy so trying harder, being more successful or having lots of friends cannot remove it. The kinds of experience that lead to shame are not always obvious, which makes it harder to understand. They may be things you had little control over such as an illness or the breakdown of a marriage but you blame yourself anyway. They can be a series of the most trivial shortcomings such as forgetting friend's birthdays or arriving late for appointments, which become entrenched in your behaviour and validate your insidious sense of shame. People-pleasing, trying to 'keep up with the Jones's' or fit into the group against your natural instinct also cultivate one's sense of shame.

Shame interferes with connectedness leading to feelings of alienation. As I said the lessening of shame comes from learning through relationships that we are all imperfect and this is okay. The best antidote is telling your story honestly and openly to others and listening to their stories to restore authentic connections that will allow empathy, compassion and love to flow again. I know this from my own experience having stood up and told the most difficult parts of my story to others over and over again. The *Spirituality of Imperfection* by Ernest Kurtz and Katherine Ketcham gives lots of examples of how this works. Shame hates it when you tell your story – it can't cope with being shared because it thrives on being a secret, hidden part of your mind; it tells you it is protecting you so you feel like hanging onto it.

I often say to friends that the most important insight I was given by my teachers was an understanding of the meaning of pride. Selfish pride is the backstop for shame and during my earlier life it held me captive in an uncomfortable prison that my mind had created. In this place you are cut off from other people so you can create self-centred stories and blame the outsiders until one day you realise that they don't have the key to your cell – it is on your side of the door. I now believe that your first act must be to open up after which it is the connection with other people that works the magic of social engagement and shared meaning and you can begin to let go of your suffering.

Envy and jealousy are two common instruments of suffering. The former concerns things that others have that you would like; the latter stems from the possibility of losing something that you are strongly attached to because you think someone else wants to take it away from you. These emotions affect men and women differently as was evident in an experiment to test the effects of overt flirting by a male or female experimenter in a large group of people. When the women were being attracted by an appealing man their male partners tended to withdraw and sulk. When it was the men being attracted by a pretty girl the women tended to get closer and even hold on to their partners.

Fear is a healthy primary emotion that keeps our mind alert yet most of us are not really comfortable with it because it often seems to overplay its hand or come to the fore when it is not actually needed. Even when things are going well we are inclined to worry and the greater the desire to control the future the more intense the worry becomes. There has been a massive increase in the diagnosis of anxiety disorders from 4% of the population in 1980 to 25% in 2010 across several countries including Australia. Some experts suggest that the more stringent diagnostic criteria have contributed to this by including everybody who has a naturally anxious temperament in the category of the mentally ill. Allan Horwitz and Jerome Wakefield wrote *All We Have To Fear – Psychiatry's Transformation of Natural Anxiety into Mental Disorders* to explain this viewpoint. Another contributing factor could be our greater reliance on left-brain activity bringing a narrower focus and a less confident relationship with the unknown. It is unrealistic to expect to live without some anxiety as Rollo May pointed out in *The Meaning of Anxiety*; it's an essential tool for our mind to function well.

Grief is a primary emotion from which there is no escape because it stems from the loss of what we need most – a loving connection. Our life drives us towards meaningful connections, but sadly, they don't last forever. When we lose a loved one or a friend we simply have to endure pain and sorrow for a time. The imagination keeps coming up with fleeting possibilities that are dashed a moment later when you realise the person involved is no longer there. In time this fades and the intensity of the suffering lessens. Such is our need for social engagement that a 'broken heart' can be just as painful as a broken leg – in fact exactly the same brain hormones are involved and the same painkillers provide relief. Bereavement used to be excluded from the diagnosis of depression but the feelings are so similar that now it is included – with rather arbitrary time limits.

The state that we call sadness is an enigma. It isn't always seen as a negative emotion even though it's an unpleasant feeling. Writers and composers have captured, through their poetic expression, a considerable beauty attached to sadness. Shakespeare described parting as 'sweet sorrow' and nostalgia is a melancholy tinged with pleasure or satisfaction. Karla McLaren sees sadness as a blessed release providing a life-giving fluidity and helping you to come to terms with reality. Christophe André feels that sadness is needed at times but it's a mistake to overvalue it.

In ancient times the melancholic (black bile) was one of four possible states of mind, the others being choleric (yellow bile), phlegmatic (phlegm) and sanguine (blood), named after the supposedly basic fluids of life. The idea was that each of us has different proportions of these four elements. The conundrum that has existed forever is: how are we to distinguish between melancholy as a mere temperament and melancholia as an illness that requires treatment? Hippocrates' suggestion over 2000 years ago that we see how long it lasts is still the criterion for the diagnosis of depression today so we still have the question: how long is too long for sadness to continue?

Depression is a clinical condition in which the feeling of meaninglessness and futility takes over one's mind completely for a long period. The World Health Organisation rates it as rapidly becoming the most prevalent form of suffering in the entire world! It is not confined to affluent Western society. It is so widespread and ideas about its causation are so varied and vague that it is one of the most baffling medical issues. In a comprehensive book that is also powerfully personal called *The Noonday Demon*, Andrew Solomon suggests that, at best, it will only ever be contained. Treatment by medication can be helpful, but the results are inconsistent, probably because no particular chemical imbalance in the brain or body has been definitely proved to be the cause. Evidence for the role of serotonin, for example, is not conclusive. Jonathan Rottenberg wrote *The Depths – The Evolutionary Origins of the Depression Epidemic* in which he advocates moving away from the simplistic paradigm of a chemical imbalance to look at the evolutionary development of this condition and its broader causes in modern society.

Clinical depression is much more commonly recognised since 1980 in many countries (doubling in the US) and some research found a correlation with the loss of interpersonal cohesion (connectedness) that is especially evident in immigrant populations whose living standards have improved, but at the expense of their close family ties. Surveys of the level of happiness in different populations have never been very convincing, but their most consistent finding is that the best predictor of perceived happiness is the prevalence of close-knit small groups of individuals within that population. Long-term studies such as the Harvard Longitudinal Study suggest strongly that it is the warmth and quality of the interpersonal relationships that best protects people against depression over their lifetime. Yet we all know people who seem to have warm, close relationships but are suffering from depression.

Rates of depression are increasing more rapidly in the younger members of the population and the reasons for that are not clear. Clinical depression affects many more women than men; males are more likely to deny it and deflect it with other symptoms like increased anger and irritability. There is considerable disagreement amongst the experts about whether the classification system for mental illness (the Diagnostic and Statistical Manual of Mental Disorders or DSM) has contributed to the over-diagnosis of depression. Allan Horwitz and Jerome Wakefield wrote *The Loss of Sadness – How Psychiatry Transformed Normal Sorrow into Depressive Illness* to debate this issue. This is an important question because people suffering from depression have many treatment options to choose from and some of the most effective such as physical exercise, yoga and mindfulness practice are quite amenable to self-management.

The pursuit of happiness may itself be a subtle cause of suffering. What Russ Harris called *The Happiness Trap* is the mistaken belief that happiness is the natural default state for human beings so everyone else is presumably in that state and the fact that I'm not enjoying it right now shows that something must be wrong with me. This is another example of the value of accepting whatever feelings come along without comparing them with anybody else – trusting in the fact that they will turn into something else. This is what doesn't happen if you are severely depressed.

Resentment – the re-feeling of anger – is a particularly insidious and destructive element of suffering. It is the remanence aspect of anger that comes from ruminating on it instead of moving on with your life. There is no good evidence that letting off steam through anger has any physiological benefits. Occasional anger may be useful if it clears the air but there is no such thing as a useful resentment. If angry feelings persist or arise frequently the reactivity of the egoic self is the prime culprit. Resentment is often accompanied by self-pity as it was in my case.

There will always be disagreeable aspects of our experience and, just as stress can be demanding without necessarily being experienced as suffering, our best hope is that these annoyances could be regarded as normal consequences of the challenging task of being and belonging. To want to be totally comfortable and insulated from the flux of life would be to disown life itself. Yet the experience of suffering is a universally unpleasant aspect of the everyday use of our mind that cannot be denied – or fully explained.

When we suffer it is normal to turn our mind towards the possibility of changing something in our mind and our lives so we will feel better.

# Chapter 16

# Courage to Change

Let's face it – we are creatures of habit. Aristotle asks in his *Nicomachean Ethics* whether we do what we do primarily because of our nature, our instruction or our habits and concludes that habit is the strongest of the three. William James, one of the founding fathers of psychology, apparently described his own life as a 'mass of habits.' When I ask myself how many of my actions are fresh decisions that I make on the spot and how many are comfortable habits I find the answer a bit disturbing. At least the habits I have now are not as debilitating as those that sabotaged the early part of my life – and eventually had to be changed.

Habits are not easy to change. Suffering would seem to be a good reason to change but it isn't a simple matter even if the habits are causing pain. Sometimes people don't want to give up the pleasure that accompanies the suffering, others can't see any alternative anyway and some habits take on an addictive force that seems to be impossible to overcome. I reached a stage where I really *wanted* to change. This was significant because the chief characteristic of comfortable habits is that we don't want to change them. They become an in-built part of who we have decided we are – like Henry Higgins delusion about his great virtues. The more comfortable the habit the less we notice its effect although others might see it quite differently.

So the essential prerequisite is a *willingness* to change, which is also an authentic *acceptance* of the present situation and of what needs to happen. Here we are revisiting the distinction between the two driving forces that are our wants and our needs. The first reaction to suffering, as with stress itself, is to want to turn away from it, to deny it or judge it – anything but accept it. We can avoid external physical threats by moving away but what is happening to our mind as a whole can't be brushed off without leaving its mark. That is how stress builds up over time and starts to cause damage. The same principle applies to suffering – it is made worse by denying it or turning away.

The hardest thing to face is the fact that we hurt most where we care most. What hurts and what we care about occupy the same place in our mind – they are bound together. The practice of love is the most painful aspect of mind as well as the most satisfying. To never hurt would be to never love (or live for that matter). Aliveness is an engagement with the world that prompts us to keep on connecting wholeheartedly, which means dealing with all issues as they come up and utilising loving relationships wherever possible to help us get through.

Throughout history many people have used their suffering as a catalyst for change – even as the trigger for a major turning point or transformation in their lives – and they have changed in ways that wouldn't have happened if they hadn't suffered in the first place. I used the example of Eckhart Tolle previously. Steven Hayes from the University of Nevada had a crippling anxiety disorder as a young man and he used this experience to develop therapeutic principles that he calls 'psychological flexibility,' which became known as Acceptance-Commitment-Therapy or ACT. One of many books about this is called *Get Out of Your Mind and Into Your Life* by Steven Hayes and Spenser Smith. An Australian therapist, Russ Harris, outlines the process in his popular book *The Happiness Trap*.

Finding the willingness to change is the acceptance part of ACT. Hayes makes the important point that the language in which our thoughts are constructed is an obstacle to change because we mistake the thought we have for the reality of what we are describing. This reminds me of Alan Watts in *The Wisdom of Insecurity* saying: 'we suffer from the delusion that the entire universe is held in order by the categories of human thought.' Our story and the language we use are only commentaries on reality, not the experience itself – they are more like what is written on the menu than the meal itself.

Hayes calls this language problem 'cognitive fusion' and advocates a process of 'defusion' in order to reframe one's meaning-making process. Our thoughts have a logical consistency because of our left-brain process and they prove themselves to be correct in such a convincing way that we can't see beyond them or that the language may have distorted the reality of our situation. This is where it is helpful to be talking with other people about it because they may see the reality more clearly.

Cognitive defusion is a process of separating your thoughts from their referents. One suggestion for doing this is to say them in a funny voice (like the chipmunks, for example) or sing them in a song. Importantly, I think, Hayes adds a form of mindfulness to this process and emphasises the present-moment experience as a way of seeing things more clearly. This will take the emphasis away from the thoughts and allow your whole mind, especially the feeling, to express itself in a more complete way. The meaning we make with our whole mind is not simplistically judgmental and controlling – it has a different quality when it includes the part I call soul that knows love. Steven Hayes uses the word 'love' a lot and his catchphrase is 'love is not everything, it's the only thing.'

Acceptance is different from simply admitting something intellectually. It means to take what is being offered to you, which we can only do if we have a sense of willingness and that seems to stem more from our heart than our head. Willingness to change is not the same as wanting something specific, it is not conditional or manipulative, it is not even trying – it is more like being prepared to jump in the deep end of a pool you've never been in before. It includes trust in the unknown so it involves our subconscious and is most evident in the in-between realm of our mind that is our feelings.

The commitment part of ACT refers to 'values-based living' and Hayes speaks about values as chosen life directions or ways of living your life. They are not goals or outcomes and are not situated somewhere in the future – they are how you want to be today. We can work out how we want to live today by asking ourselves what value or principle is it that my life will serve today. We are all living to serve something or someone. To live according to your values – not just to achieve certain outcomes – leads to a less manipulative and more reflective lifestyle.

A more mechanistic approach to change is found in Charles Duhigg's book *The Power of Habit*. He suggests there is a simple formula by which we can change any of our habits; whether it works or not still depends on our willingness. The same process by which the learned emotional responses became habitual in the first place brings about the change. Each habit is a behavioural routine that is triggered by one or more cues and delivers some kind of reward – both the cues and the reward are feelings. When the reward feeling is strong enough to set up a craving, even a mild one, the habit has been formed. If you can identify the specific cues and attach them to a different behaviour that delivers the same or similar feelings of reward your habit will be changed.

Mechanistic or not I know this does work – if you can pro-actively manage your feelings, trust in the unknown and don't try to figure it out – you just do it. At first you don't feel like substituting the new behaviour for the old one because you doubt that it will work as well and it feels uncomfortable. The force of habit in your mind will tell you to go back to the old behaviour but if you persevere, your feelings may give you a glimmer of hope that the reward is reachable in this new way. Being with other people in similar situations is a great help. The crucial part is *doing, not thinking*. I was unable to think my way into a better way of life, but as I started to trust something larger than myself I became prepared to do things differently and thankfully, I kept this up until some new habits were formed.

This is also the way my friend Alastair finally broke free from his debilitating habits that made his life so grim at the beginning of this book. He says it was out of desperation in the end that he joined in with a group of people who were helping one another to introduce some different habits into their routine behaviour. I see him from time to time and it fills my heart with gladness to see the authentic Alastair whom I always tried to love shining through. He says he still doesn't agree with me about the unknown, but I'm not absolutely sure he means that! He always asks me when this book will be finished and I tell him that it will soon be drawing to a close.

When this method of change doesn't work Duhigg says that what is lacking is *belief*. He gives examples of how two sporting teams practice the plays that will win games, but when they are evenly matched, the result seems to depend on the subconscious belief the players have in themselves and in what they are doing, which means they don't have to think about it – they just feel it and do it. Whether it is in a team sport or a self-help community the emotional bond between the participants strengthens their belief.

Belief is a function of our imagination and includes respect for the unknown. Perhaps the reason we don't believe we can change is that we fear to let ourselves go to a place where we are worthy enough to deserve that change – where we are truly loved. Several famous people have speculated that what we fear most is success. Erich Fromm wrote about *The Fear of Freedom* that has arisen because the restrictions on individual freedom have lessened and yet we seem to miss having some kind of larger-than-self authority in our lives. This is a strange kind of fear, perhaps only really understood by our soul.

We need to involve our whole mind to find the necessary courage to change. It has little to do with that overrated ability we call willpower because it is essentially an acceptance of reality and a surrender of the mind to unknown influences followed by much practice at doing things differently. I know that is a path to freedom if you are trapped by your own mind. Feeling free is great but the feeling of becoming free is even sweeter. Change is mostly incremental, as in evolution, so we are never finished even though we recognise that both our *affect* and our *story* have moved along.

We rewrite our stories all the time, hence the great importance of conversation, but we also cling to their basic structure because that is how we make sense of our lives. If we need a drastic rewrite for our wellbeing there are some interesting ways to do this explained by Timothy Wilson in his book, *Redirect: The Surprising New Science of Psychological Change*. His research shows that some current practices that are supposed to be helpful don't work very well. Critical Incident Debriefing immediately after a traumatic experience did not help to prevent PTSD whereas calmer reflective writing at a later date allowed the emotions, feelings and thoughts to come together more effectively so the experience could be accommodated into the person's story more thoroughly.

He describes research with new University students who had received much lower marks than they expected at their first exam. Some students used this to reinforce their story that they probably weren't cut out for University. Subsequently their work rate fell away, their results deteriorated and they dropped out. Other students had a more positive and confident story that they must not have worked hard enough for that exam and it seemed that being at University was going to require more effort than they had expected. Their story did not include the expectation of failure.

It doesn't help to tell the negative students that their story could be wrong and they should change it. But when some groups in Wilson's research were supplied, quite unobtrusively, with information showing how common it was to get low marks at first and describing the usual rate of improvement as the course progresses, those groups had significantly fewer drop-outs than matched control groups. They weren't told to think differently yet they did. Trying to tell others that their story is wrong – your teenage children for example – simply doesn't work.

Lots of research shows that large rewards are not very effective and severe punishments don't work either because they draw more attention to avoiding the punishment than to taking responsibility for your own autonomous behaviour. Mildly annoying threats and small rewards are more effective and easier to implement. Complimenting children on their success certainly helps as long as it acknowledges that it was their effort that was rewarded.

We come back to the fact that the most powerful story-editing process of all is what Wilson calls the 'do good to feel good' principle. What we do shapes our minds and our narratives immediately and sustainably so when we do something esteemable our self-esteem is enhanced. This is not simply positive thinking; it's a way of improving self-worth and connectability that creates more hopeful meanings and more purpose in life. He gives examples of reductions in delinquency, teenage pregnancy, and drug and alcohol abuse when young people were set up with opportunities for doing a small amount of volunteer work that was chosen to suit their individual temperaments. In contrast a typical scare program of taking disadvantaged children around the jails and hospitals and showing them horrible consequences of bad behaviour actually seemed to reinforce their story that perhaps it would be okay after all to be with those guys.

For changing racial or cultural prejudice he found that nothing worked better than regular contact with people who are different from yourself. Education programs, including intense workshops (such as 'Blue Eyes/Brown Eyes') designed to make you experience prejudice, seemed to achieve very little. Simply spending time together with people from different cultures had an immediate and lasting effect by creating new stories in place of the old. In that case the interpersonal connections include all levels of the mind.

Habits are such a significant part of our everyday mind and so insidious in their effect that we stand to gain if we can find the courage to examine them honestly and believe that they can be changed. This will never be a 'quick fix' because worthwhile change is incremental – it evolves. The rewards for doing so extend much deeper than our conscious mind because we are being influenced by subtle forces to do with our values and moral judgments.

# Chapter 17

# Values

We say we value some things in our lives more than others – that they are more precious or meaningful and we wouldn't like to lose them. We also speak of ideals that we aspire towards and standards that we try to uphold. It registers in our feelings whether we are true to these or not because it is a key component of the way we make meaning.

First up I described the meaning we experience as a subjective sense of satisfaction but it can also be defined in other ways and even seems to defy our attempts to say exactly what meaning means! It often denotes the significance or relevance or importance of something, which is also called its *value*. This too is an elusive concept.

The proactive nature of our perception makes it difficult for us to distinguish between some value that is intrinsic and already present in what we are observing and the value we have bestowed upon it as we perceived it. Is it simply our version of the value or do other people see it the same way? In our individualistic culture we tend towards the idea that values are largely personal preferences. At the same time most of us like to think that things exist whether we perceive them or not so in that case they presumably have a value in their own right. The more obviously we ignore this the more self-centred we become.

Two of the central themes of this book are involved here. One is the idea that meaning is not precise enough to be explained objectively, nor is it simply an emotional state or a rational idea – it arises as a whole-of-mind process and becomes most apparent in our feelings. The second is the idea foreshadowed earlier that love legitimises what we see before us and makes it real. We sometimes say that love confuses our perception by putting a gloss on it but that is the selfish imagination – an indulgence in our own pleasure. In fact we see reality most clearly through love because we have not contaminated what we see with preconceived ideas, particularly expectations of our ego.

I quoted Robert Johnson earlier saying that love is 'the power within us that affirms and values another human being as he or she is . . . at its very essence it is an appreciation – a recognition of value.' In this way it is love that enables us to appreciate value.

This was elaborated most clearly by the early 20th century German philosopher, Max Scheler. He adopted Roman Catholicism early in his life and his work was the subject of a Doctoral thesis by the man who became Pope John Paul II. Scheler distanced himself from the church later, professing a spirituality he called 'philosophical anthropology,' which he was writing about when his life was cut short at age 54 in 1928. The Nazis destroyed much of his work after he died. At the time his standing in European philosophy was very high yet I feel his work has been neglected since then.

He was a pioneer of phenomenology, though not as a formal methodology, because he described it as 'an attitude of spiritual seeing' rather than an empirical set of observations. His basic idea is that values are experienced in our feelings. He says that values are not simply feelings, they are meanings, but they reach us through feelings just as colour reaches us through sight. They are not flavours added to improve something nor are they a consequence of something else, they are the primary facts of reality. Our attention process, which determines what our world seems like to us, is guided mainly by what Scheler calls 'value-ception' – the perception of value as we understand it.

In psychology this fits with the 'primacy of affect' – the idea that the emotional impact precedes other aspects of perception and thereby forms the framework in which the meaning will arise. The central plank in this framework is what Scheler refers to as love. He suggests that love is what creates value whereas hate destroys it and I would add that cynicism and indifference will deprive us of both meaning and value. Scheler warns that egoic judgments, as distinct from value-ception, are a form of 'poison for our mind.'

In other words love is actually the reason that we have values in the first place. Scheler writes about love as our primary animation or 'movement.' It is love that enables our mind to know value because looking with love legitimises what we see. Hatred on the other hand closes off our sense of value. As he puts it: 'love and hate are acts in which the value-realm accessible to the feelings of a being . . . is either extended or narrowed.' Love and hate are not reactions – they are the very ground from which the possibility of value arises. Love is an intentional act of mind that discloses value.

We can't define value precisely because it is neither purely subjective (whatever I take it to be) nor purely consensual (whatever we agree it to be). It is pre-reflective like the subconscious component of empathy or compassion in that it comes to us before we have thought about it. What we can say about value is that it engages our attention. When we find we love doing something or being with someone we are acknowledging that we value that experience – we recognise something of value in it, subconsciously at first, then as part of our story. If we don't continue to appreciate it this value will fade from our awareness, as we know from what happens when we take good things too much for granted.

To remain part of our awareness and our story the experience of value has to consolidate its meaning over time and it is here we see that values are not all the same in terms of their effect on our wellbeing. Scheler ranks them in a hierarchy with the *utilitarian* values of practicality and basic comfort at the bottom, the *sensual* values of what is agreeable and what is disagreeable just above that, the *vital* or *life* values of what is 'noble' and what is 'vulgar' next highest, the *psychic* values of the 'ugly' or the 'beautiful' higher again and the *spiritual* values of 'holy' and 'unholy' at the top of the pyramid.

You might recognise in this description shades of Maslow's 'hierarchy of needs' that came much later in 1943 apparently without any reference to Scheler. Abraham Maslow was unusual amongst psychologists of his time because he forsook the study of mentally ill people (whose 'immaturity led to an immature psychology') and chose to study only the people he regarded as the healthiest who were the highest achievers in the population. He places *physiological* needs at the bottom; above that *safety and security* needs and above that the *social* needs of love and belonging. That leads to the second highest level, which is *self-esteem and self-confidence*. The highest level he calls *self-actualisation* in which he includes goals that are higher than oneself and for the 'greater good' such as altruism and spirituality.

In both cases there are spiritual matters at the top and more sensual and practical matters at the bottom. What is different is that Scheler is talking about values that we aspire towards whereas Maslow is talking about needs that require our attention and therefore provide the motivation for our mind to develop. Maslow says that deficiencies in the first four needs lead to anxiety and distress. Scheler emphasises the vital values (noble or vulgar) as the most common grounds for insecurity and anxiety if they are neglected.

Models such as these may guide us in finding meaning but they also distort meaning if we take them too literally. Maslow was often criticised because these categories do not exist separately even though they do describe a line of development towards wellbeing. Moving up his pyramid from the lower values towards the higher takes us from the more superficial and selfish uses of the mind towards relationships and a broader context. This could be compared to a *maturation* of the mind, which might be expected to occur throughout one's lifetime.

Another philosophical psychologist, Harry Overstreet, explains very deftly that, although we grow and change as we age, the human mind does not necessarily mature with age. He was 73 in 1949 when he published *The Mature Mind* – a best-selling book in its day and still regarded as a classic – suggesting that psychological age is not the same as chronological age and irresponsible behaviour stems from psychological immaturity. For him maturity is the progress from self-orientation to meaningful relationships. His 'linkage theory' that man lives by and through his relationships was prescient of today's social neuroscience. He says the maturing person is one whose 'linkages with life are constantly becoming stronger and richer because his attitudes are such as to encourage their growth.' He goes on to say that 'a mind grows towards maturity as it widens its relations to the not yet realised,' which I would equate with the relationship with the unknown.

If our life is a movement in search of wellbeing, which the primary emotion of *Seeking* promotes, what exactly is it we are hoping to achieve? I'm suggesting it is a satisfaction with life, which will be a set of feelings and a sense of meaning. This is not the same as continuous happiness, of course, certainly not ecstasy or bliss or mystical revelations. It is a certain amount of comfort for our mind, content with knowing that there will be pain as well as pleasure, sorrow as well as joy, and always more questions than answers. There cannot be complete satisfaction – both our feelings and meaning will always be unfinished business. When we get stuck we tend to think of ourselves as a finished product, which is not true – we are always a work in progress.

For the purpose of my book I have my own version of a **hierarchy of meaning** for the human mind, which is also a **hierarchy of feelings**. At the bottom is *physiological utility*, which is the basic autonomy and connectedness that keeps us alive – the foundation for feeling and meaning to occur. The next level I call *physical comfort*, which includes basic safety and security and the sensual pleasures or otherwise pains that are an obvious part of our everyday experience. The third level is *psychological comfort* including anxiety or peace of mind, equivalent to Scheler's vital values and very much a product of Maslow's social needs at this level. On the fourth level, *aesthetic comfort*, are feelings and meaning that only occur when our mind can distinguish what is beautiful from what is ugly. At the top is *spiritual comfort*, which is a relationship with the unknown that may bring joy or fear or is often disregarded altogether.

But once again the model is just a flimsy contraption that our left-brain logic creates as an outline and we do well to let it pass through our mind and disappear. Each of us decides what we value and what we need using our unique combination of intuition and rationality. I think it is helpful to reflect from time to time on what one's values are and how they affect one's wellbeing.

Scheler warns against 'value inversion,' which he refers to as a 'self-poisoning of the mind' that leads to negative judgments about oneself and others manifesting as disapproval, anger and passive aggression. He suggests that nothing will ever be sacred or highly valued to a self-poisoned mind. His idea of a 'self-inflicted personal sense of inadequacy' reminds me of my own worst experiences and the recurring theme of not knowing that you are loved. Scheler foresaw, at a time when neuroscience and psychology were much less developed than they are today, that the values that our mind believes in and is guided by bring about the kind of experience that we are having. I equate his idea of value inversion with the improper use of my mind.

Tied in with our sense of values are our ideas about ethics and our moral judgments, both of which are big subjects in their own right. I can sum up what I have to say about ethics by referring back to the biology – whether something is life-promoting or life-destroying. Much of what is happening by way of the destruction of our environment, antisocial and hateful behaviour is unethical without any doubt. Mankind is its own worst enemy in this regard.

Our sense of meaning is shaped a lot by the moral judgments that we make. These are part of our personal values so they predispose our attention towards some things and away from others and are a major factor in the shared meaning within a group. This works to bind our societies together in a beneficial way, while at the same time it is what produces most of the division and antagonism between different societies. This is described by Harvard psychology professor, Joshua Greene, in his book *Moral Tribes*. He says there are two kinds of moral problem: 'me versus us' which is the being and belonging I have been describing here and 'us versus them' which is the issue of tribal conflict. He explains (as I have) that our biology equips us to deal with the first issue well enough. He is more pessimistic about the tribal conflict, which he says can only be solved rationally – if we can manage to negotiate rationally!

Our mind by its nature is *The Righteous Mind*, which is the title of another book by Jonathan Haidt. He said he could have called the book 'the moral mind,' but that would not have conveyed the idea that we are 'intrinsically critical and judgmental.' His point is that this kind of mind made it possible for human beings to form large, cooperative societies in which altruism abounds while at the same time guaranteeing that, between these different groups, there will always be moralistic strife. Morality 'binds us and blinds us' he says.

The classical explanation for moral judgment describes it as a 'dual process' arising from both emotion and reason. However, Jonathan Haidt's first principle of moral psychology is that 'intuition comes first, moral reasoning second' and the latter is used to justify the former. He developed a 'social intuitionist' model of moral judgment in which 'the intuitive dog wags the rational tail.' Our adaptive unconscious makes quick and quite rigid judgments which our conscious mind then rationalises and justifies after the event. Its main motivation for doing this is to satisfy the requirements of social relationships. Haidt gives examples of how we are all quite like 'politicians' in that it is more important to look good and fit in than it is to be absolutely honest. We lie so well we believe what we are saying, which will generally be whatever supports our 'team' best.

A strong feeling that is related to our morals and values is *disgust* that originates in the insula region of our brain where our sense of self is also based. It could almost be a primary emotion except that it is culturally acquired and people learn in different cultures to find different things disgusting.

The feeling of disgust is highly contagious and, like fear, it can be communicated through smell at a subconscious level. While it may have originated to guard us against ingesting contaminated food or drink, it seems to have a more subtle role in turning us away from behaviours that make us feel bad in a moral or ethical sense. A leading researcher in this field, Paul Rozin thinks this may be to do with our sense of ourselves as animals. The only bodily products that humans don't feel disgusted by are tears, which are also the only ones that other animals don't produce. We know we are related to other animals but we associate our humanness with qualities other than the animal ones, which are more likely to arouse our sense of shame.

Perhaps the hierarchy of values I have discussed here is also based on our sense of humanness being a special quality that transcends our biology, even though it is built on it. In seeking to go beyond physical and psychological comfort we are reaching into realms that imply spirituality in that they seem to draw us towards the unknown. Yet there is surely a great need for aesthetic and spiritual comfort to nourish our soul.

## Chapter 18

# A Need for Beauty

My friend Rachael goes into raptures whenever she sees a bloom of new flowers or a stunning pattern on a dress or even a small green frog for that matter. She is captivated by colour and form and seems to experience beauty with her whole body and mind. I must confess that she notices it where I often miss it – for example in a tiny native bluebell that hides itself along a bush track near where we both live. Rachael's garden is designed to have something in flower all year round so she has azaleas, camellias, rhododendrons, lavender, winter pansies, spring bulbs, petunias and so on, along with our native gems like kangaroo paw, grevilleas and waratah.

There is beauty everywhere in nature that we may or may not attend to depending on the priorities we establish in our minds. Around here it is in sandstone cliffs, waterfalls, sweeping valleys and shady, secluded glens that surprise you as you walk alongside mountain streams and feel the mighty canopy of trees above you. I love trees and I find that walking in the forest never fails to excite something in my mind that is an extra layer of value, enhancing psychological comfort as it extends beyond it.

Our sense of beauty is a mysterious aspect of mind yet who among us has not experienced it or does not desire it in some form? If we didn't I wonder whether there would be any satisfaction and wellbeing? Sir Roger Scruton, who probably writes more about beauty than any other philosopher, says that our intuitive appreciation of beauty is so absolutely essential for our mind that if we lost it we would not be human. He believes it is the crux of our pursuit of meaning and says that if its influence declines our wellness will suffer.

That it is built into our biology is explained by another distinguished philosopher of the arts, Stephen Davies, in a book called *The Artful Species – Aesthetics, Art and Evolution*. He says that 'aesthetic responses and art behaviours are the touchstones of our humanity.' Denis Dutton who wrote *The Art Instinct - Beauty, Pleasure and Human Evolution* also came to the conclusion that our artistic tendencies are basic instincts that we've had for a long time.

They both believe that very early humans must have had an 'aesthetic sensibility' – a taste for the creation and appreciation of beauty. This is evident in early musical instruments, in stone axes found at burial sites that are honed and polished for their colour, sheen and shape far beyond functional necessity, and also in the great lengths taken to produce elaborate cave art in very inaccessible places. Davies dismisses the idea that the aesthetic sense was an accidental by-product of our evolution as suggested by Steven Pinker and a few other prominent neuroscientists. It has surely been a crucial part of our evolutionary progress that guided the development of those higher values that are distinctively human elements of our mind.

Aesthetics is not simply a feeling of pleasure – you can get good feelings from being praised or massaged or eating fine food and you would value these at a more superficial level, but in art you are appreciating another dimension of value. Davies says that 'aesthetic experience is an 'attention-focussing, value-charged response' that affects our mind through feelings.

Although some people try to describe beauty in terms of purely objective properties, I think the most plausible explanations about our aesthetic sensibilities go in the opposite direction by acknowledging the mystery of this kind of experience. John O'Donohue, in a book called *Divine Beauty - The Invisible Embrace*, says the experience of beauty seems to come from beyond what we think we know. To notice it we need to acknowledge the incompleteness of our knowing. Beauty calls forth the integrity of our experience just as love reveals the value that our mind naturally seeks. An American poet, Frederick Turner, calls beauty 'the highest integrative level of understanding.'

O'Donohue further describes beauty as a wealth that we often neglect. He argues that 'much of the stress and emptiness that haunts us can be traced back to our lack of attention to beauty.' Our mind naturally seeks it everywhere but we often mistake glamour for beauty and glamour is only skin deep. The very first effect it has on your mind is the only effect it will ever have whereas beauty is an invitation into a deeper world of meaning, knowing that you are alive for reasons other than productivity and consumption. He says that our hunger for beauty is the feeling of our soul embracing the unknown.

Because beauty happens in our experience it has to be noticed so our appreciation of it depends on where we choose to direct our attention. Iain McGilchrist believes that the left side of our brain is designed to give us the most explicit kind of meaning and in doing so it denies us the experience of beauty. He believes that 'explicitness kills, renders lifeless.' It is our right brain that gives us context rather than abstraction, flow instead of fixity and the ability to see visual depth in art and hear harmony in music. McGilchrist warns that undue reliance on our left brain has neutralised the power of the arts so that, as he puts it, 'beauty has been airbrushed out.'

We use our right brain to appreciate nuances of facial expression. Before the 6th century BC, the faces depicted in art are expressionless and stare straight ahead, but after that, McGilchrist says, most paintings show faces looking towards the viewer's left. This emphasises the subject's left side (right brain) and puts the focus of attention in the viewer's left visual field (also the right brain). He found in his research that this greater use of the right hemisphere disappeared in the Dark Ages, reappeared in the Renaissance, and has now disappeared again. He attributes the great surge in creative arts generally after the 6th century BC to a period of right brain dominance in human history. This was also the beginning of the Greek philosophy that shaped Western culture so strongly.

The growth and spread of literacy engaged more left brain activity and heightened the tension between knowing the world as a hard fact and understanding it subconsciously in terms of myth and metaphor. Descartes, in the 16th century, solidified the division between a rational mind and our bodily experience. With the Age of Enlightenment (the Age of Reason) from the 18th century we progressed to modernism and the rapid growth of science bringing an even stronger demand for certainty. Then with post-modernism, McGilchrist feels, 'meaning drains away.' He suggests that our perception of art has become more self-conscious, seeing what our superficial mind thinks should be there rather than the work itself. This is especially true of music, he says, which typifies our increasing reliance on self-perpetuating technology – a lot of today's music sounds, or is, machine-made.

Roger Scruton is even more challenging in his remarks about the diminishing awareness of beauty in the world. He says that without conscious attention to beauty we experience desecration by default. To attend to beauty we need to direct our attention away from selfish gratification towards something that makes us feel good about ourselves and our fellow humans. All our addictions, in which he includes pornography, stem from living in selfish fantasy and it's actually quite hard to escape the 'stimulus addiction' that is the stock-in-trade of TV and other mass media today. Scruton deplores the realism of modern action films that he thinks are designed to produce an immediate emotional effect without much need for imagination. To find meaning you need more than immediate effect because you need to appreciate some broader context.

While these warnings are probably timely, I think the fundamental need we have to nourish our soul is such that we will continue to find beauty in the modern world and the arts will remain very much alive. The arts stimulate our imagination because our mind is searching for value and then the quality of our looking influences what we are likely to see. It is an attitude of love that will reveal for us the true beauty in the world around us and thereby strengthen our relationships with ourselves, with others and with the unknown.

Appreciating the arts is not separate from our primary task of human connectedness. In fact the extraordinary intimacy that we humans have evolved probably came about because we were also developing our artistic instincts. Ellen Dissanayake wrote *Art and Intimacy - How the Arts Began* to show that intimacy (or love) and art (the arts) evolved together. Her idea is that love is expressed and exchanged through patterns of social engagement that she calls 'rhythms and modes,' beginning with the mother-infant relationship. Through these repetitive interactions (looks, sounds and touches) a human being learns to love and to be loved and while doing this we also learn to create little works of art that consist of rhythms and modes. Love and art are both invitations to play, which attracts us to them.

John Keats, whose life spanned only 25 years, wrote in an *Ode to a Grecian Urn*, beautiful words that evoke the deep meaning that we call *truth* as the companion of beauty:

'*Heard melodies are sweet, but those unheard*
*Are sweeter; therefore, ye soft pipes, play on*
*Not to the sensual ear, but, more endear'd*
*Pipe to the spirit ditties of no tone.*'

'*Beauty is truth, truth beauty – that is all*
*Ye know on earth, and all ye need to know.*'

# Chapter 19

# Story, Song and Music

Since the day this book began my mind and I have been experiencing *affect* and creating a *story*, some of which you have read on these pages. Everyone's story is different but there are common threads of meaning that have been captured by storytellers down through the ages. I relate to *Parsifal* and his search for the Holy Grail because I have been trying to explain how mind affects wellbeing based on my own experience and I realise how far my explanation falls short of its ideal – yet there is also consolation in this story for me.

I liken my dark times to the kind of woundedness that Robert Johnson calls, in *The Fisher King*, the damaged 'feeling function,' which he says is 'the most common and painful wound' in the Western world and the most dangerous because it goes unrecognised. As in many stories about a male's haphazard journey towards maturity I rode out with princely hopes of winning battles only to lose my way in my 20's and 30's. In the classic story The Fisher King lives in constant misery in the Grail castle and *Parsifal*, whose name means Innocent Fool, gains access to the castle in his young life but leaves again without having asked the crucial question that would heal the King and all his realm. The story is about finding a true power. In later life, after much travail, *Parsifal* enters the castle again and asks the question – 'whom does the Grail serve' – which reveals the Higher Power that is the healing force. Failure to acknowledge this power that is greater than oneself that I call the unknown is one way we neglect the feeling aspect of our mind.

Robert Johnson says in *The Handless Maiden* that the wounded feeling function is felt by women more symbolically in their hands – their cry is 'what can I do?' Our society has made it difficult for women to work out what to do to express the power they already possess. It was actually a 'devil's bargain' by a miller to buy new technology to make his life easier that led, without him realising it, to the loss of his daughter's hands; the wound strikes women while they are young. The story of healing includes a time in the forest alone, the act of saving a baby's life in a river, and silver hands that become real. My oversimplification demeans the rich qualities of these stories, but I hope it illustrates the enormous power that stories have in shaping our minds.

Famous stories have changed the course of history. Biographies of Adolf Hitler describe how he was besotted with the music and the ideas of Richard Wagner, whose opera *Rienzi* had influenced him greatly as a young man. It is about a powerful Roman leader on whom Hitler modelled himself. Amongst the best-selling books of the 19<sup>th</sup> century was *Uncle Tom's Cabin*, which polarised American society and triggered huge cultural change regarding slavery just as *To Kill a Mocking Bird* changed racial attitudes around the world a century later. These are just a few examples amongst many. Even more powerful perhaps are the various creation myths of different ethnic groups and the ancient love stories such as *Tristan and Iseult* and *Psyche and Eros*.

My story makes up a large part of my mind but if it was only my story and you could see no sign of yourself anywhere in it we would have difficulty connecting. It's not that you and I are the same; just that we recognise similarities and these point our mind towards shared meaning. You might think we'd be better served by stories that were literally true but by far the greater part of our storytelling is what we call fiction.

In *The Storytelling Animal – How Stories Made us Human* Jonathan Gottschall says that we hardly realise how bewitched we are by stories. We immerse ourselves in stories told by others in blogs, books, films and theatre and, in our conversation, we shape our own story around everything else. It is said that fiction is escapist but why would we want to escape into imaginary lives that are even more difficult than our own? Gottschall thinks we learn from this. People who read a lot of fiction were found to be better problem-solvers than those who didn't, particularly around social situations.

Personal memoirs are important because they help us to see that fiction and 'true' stories are not really very different. All stories are made up because they stem from our imperfect memories and are held together by figments of our imagination, but they are always 'based on a true story.' Good writers tend to be sparing or selective with detail or use universal symbols so that we, the readers, have to create our own version of the characters and the situations in the form that is most realistic for us.

Narrative imagining is a special feature of the human mind. Mark Turner, an American cognitive scientist, shows in *The Literary Mind – The Origins of Thought and Language* how our mind makes literary connections across space and time. Storytelling is not just entertainment or performance, it is the way our mind operates – the way we plan, predict and explain. It is a game of 'playing with patterns' that helps us to share meaning – a social attunement arising from play.

This ability we have to build bridges in our mind between different concepts by recognising broad similarities of form and pattern is the reason that we love metaphors, similes and analogies. Precise meanings keeps us separate whereas 'fuzzy logic' gives our mind enough room to move to find shared meaning with others. Simple logic is like a little torch we carry in the darkness to light up certain features; sharing meaning is more complex than that. Where your meaning meets mine there is a conceptual twilight in which our minds are more often groping towards one another than marching in step in broad daylight.

An integral companion of story throughout our history has been song. It's fairly certain that humans have been singing and dancing together for a very long time, possibly ever since we rose onto two legs, because that freed us up to move quite differently. Steven Mithen who wrote *The Singing Neanderthal* is amongst those anthropologists who believe that singing was important for our language development. Recent research shows that there is more of the bonding hormone, oxytocin, and better synchronisation of brainwaves, when people are singing together than is found in the same people in any other social situation. The elitism that distinguishes professional singers from amateurs nowadays has killed off old customs such as family singing around the piano though our need for it is still evident in the proliferation of community choirs.

The way we appreciate music is an exemplar of meaning-making in general being easier to capture in feelings than in words. Tonal images that we hear are more subtle but they are no less important than visual images. The senses of sight and touch tend to dominate so we need hearing to remind us that there is more to our world than what we can see or physically handle; heard images are less precise and therefore may include a greater sense of the unknown. Whereas sight draws us out into the world, hearing lets the world come in.

Oliver Sacks suggests in *Musicophilia* that we are a musical species as well as a linguistic one and our love of music is our sense of aliveness because music 'feels almost like a living thing.' We feel this in our mind's sense of movement. People with dementia or partial paralysis due to brain damage can often find themselves dancing gracefully when some music that they know is played. Mark Johnson gives examples in *The Meaning in the Body* including a commentary on the song, *Something*, which George Harrison created for the Beatles. 'Something in the way she moves, attracts me like no other lover . . .' is written so that the pitch moves, the duration of each note moves, the girl moves and you feel moved. If you rearrange the notation slightly this effect is lost and it's difficult, if not impossible, to explain why this is so.

Music helps us to understand wholeness and emergent properties because it is not the individual tones, it is their flowing combination that we appreciate and this is not a summation, of course, it is an entirely new creation whose properties could not be found in the separate components. The harmonic combination of a chord evokes our sense of space as the melody does for our sense of time.

My own desire to write songs and perform them as part of my teaching and learning did not stem from any formal training in music. It simply satisfied a need in me to find a greater shared meaning than I could obtain from scientific explanation. Maturana was very gracious when I sang songs about autopoiesis at some of his workshops. The idea behind *Stress: The Musical* is also the general idea of this book – that the 'disagreements between our insides and our outsides' that we experience as stress are best dealt with by the connectedness we feel for one another. One musical metaphor I employed was an interruption to the melodic flow of a song to show how blockages in our social engagement exacerbate stress. Another was a conflict of tempo to show how cross-currents interfere with the flow of meaning between us. The show ends in a dance with balloons. Performing this show I learned about play as a dimension of mind way beyond any scientific explanation and I felt the magical pleasure of laughing, crying and dancing together with others.

## Chapter 20

# The Feeling of Meaning

Today we will experience whatever life has in store for us. For some of what happens there is a scientific explanation, but much of it can only be explained as our first-person experience. I have tried to bridge this gap by situating the mind within our basic biology, emphasising its feeling function and drawing attention to the feeling of meaning. My explanation of mind combines science and subjective experience.

The validity of any explanation depends not so much on its self-consistency but on whether the person who hears or reads that explanation accepts it or not – whether it fits their story about their own experience. An explanation is only as good as its audience thinks it is because our meaning is our reality and that is a personal, subjective experience. Our minds make meaning to satisfy something that is primarily a feeling. The abstraction of it plays a part but it is not the endpoint.

Satisfying meaning will include many experiences that are not explained by science and these are the most precious. Aliveness includes loving others, hoping and longing, awe and wonder, pleasure from beauty in music, art and story, the pain of separation and the fear of dying. The sum of our feelings is the ever-changing barometer of our being and belonging.

People explain their experiences in many weird and wonderful ways, which the purists refer to as 'subjective idealism.' From the 'divine wisdom' of Theosophy and other 'channelled' texts through to current models of consciousness based on quantum physics we try to explain everything that happens to us. There are thousands of personal accounts of mysterious aspects of mind such as telepathy, healing at a distance, near-death journeys and other evidence suggesting that there may be a single mind of which one's own mind is just a part. But we can't have another person's experience – we can only have our own.

A common thread in all this is the idea of love. John Makransky's book *Awakening Through Love* and Thich Nhat Hanh's short books about love are practical Buddhist-based exercises in the kind of love that I have found seems to work in my own life. *A Course in Miracles* is a channelled text with explicit Christian references that became widely known when it was popularised by Marianne Williamson in *A Return to Love*. It contains spiritual principles that I also found very useful. In this approach love is described as an energy or transcendental force that comes from God. My language is a bit different in that I don't know what it is and I call its source the unknown. Thinking of mind as part of my biology I come to the conclusion that love would be what we need most. I describe love as an indispensable facilitator for the human mind.

My experience affirms this belief and I think the biological science I've outlined here supports the idea. Everything that is important to human beings seems to depend on love. It is an attitude that obviously works. As long as our motivation is narrowed by brittle self-concern we are incapable of achieving the connectedness that our aliveness requires. Love must be already there because it is available to anyone at any time – all we have to do is notice it and practice it. Our view of it is obscured by narrow patterns of selfish thoughts that label others instead of seeing them for who they are and try to control a life process that will flow anyway if we have complete confidence in it. I came to believe that we are spiritual beings simply because we are a part of something that is bigger and more powerful than ourselves. I recognise kindness and dignity as hallmarks of our humanness.

This is felt as my meaning and so it is my attitude to life. I think the worst times of one's life are the best catalysts for learning how to use one's mind and understanding the importance of attitude. Nobody shows this more clearly than Viktor Frankl who used his terrible experience as a prisoner in Nazi death camps during World War II to develop a new branch of psychology in which meaning was given top priority. In *Man's Search for Meaning* he introduced the ideas of 'logotherapy,' saying that it is not our will to pleasure nor our will to power that is fundamental – it is our will to meaning. He says our mind's first concern is to obtain a sense of meaning and this is not achieved via pleasure or power but only by actualising our values. Emphasising love, he speaks about the soul and an 'ultimate meaning' that is unattainable yet it still needs to be taken into account.

An essential element of logotherapy is to exercise the freedom to choose your attitude to whatever is happening, which he knew from his own experience is the last freedom left when all the others have been taken away. He says the 'seed of meaning' is always there but it will be harder to see if you are not attending to what is happening in the present moment. The ability to focus on and relate to what is other than ourselves is crucial along with the humility to know that we belong to something bigger.

The feeling of meaning is not the same as the feeling of knowing. In a book called *On Being Certain*, Robert Burton warns about the danger of assuming certainty and the fundamentalism that flows from that. He points out that, despite how certainty feels, it is not an act of reasoning, nor is it even a conscious choice. It's an involuntary preconception that needs to be tempered by humility – the realisation that we know only a little and our ability to judge or control anything is actually very limited. The feeling that what you know is just sufficient for this moment can be a quiet self-assurance, trusting the unknown. To think that what you know now applies to everyone and everything will be a dangerous delusion.

We often misunderstand problems that arise because we don't recognise the contribution that our feelings make to the meaning. We look first for a logical, mechanical solution to any problem and if we can't find one we often persist in analysing those same details over and over again without realising that the problem actually exists in our feelings. If we were not feeling bad about it, at least for the time being, the problem would disappear. This is the freedom we have to care properly for our feelings and choose where we direct our attention.

It is in what we do rather than what we think that we find meaning arising in our feelings. Irving Yalom puts it this way in his delightful book *Love's Executioner*: 'The search for meaning, much like the search for pleasure, must be conducted obliquely. Meaning ensues from meaningful activity. It is a by-product of engagement and commitment.' He says we need the capacity to tolerate uncertainty to do this – that the strength of our human spirit lies in a 'meaningful uncertainty.' Our feeling of meaning is never without a sense of mystery. I have tried to show that the best possible use of our mind boils down to acknowledging the mystery and devoting our attention to our connectedness at every level – with the unknown, with ourselves, with other people and with our world.

A large body of evidence that this really does work comes from the Harvard Study of Adult Development that followed hundreds of people for over 50 years to see how they responded to the ups and downs of life. As well as physical records and health history the researchers documented feelings and emotions. One of the supervising psychiatrists was George Vaillant who wrote *Spiritual Evolution – How We Are Wired for Faith, Hope and Love*. He says he learned from this study that faith, hope and love express themselves through people's attitudes. Our negative emotions are important at the time they happen, but in the long run it is the positive emotions from which we gain the meaning we need. He describes these positive emotions as an attitude of 'spirituality' (from the Latin for breath) which, he says, like breathing, simply means 'participating in life.'

Many of our worries stem from the selfish and destructive behaviour of other people including some large groups of people who think they know what others should believe and do. It's a fact that some of our fellow human beings want to subvert and kill others so we may have to fight to survive. Humberto Maturana pioneered 'cultural biology' in showing that our cultural outcomes will depend on what state of mind people are preserving and what state of mind we are neglecting over a period of time. If we neglect love, beauty and spirituality while preserving power struggles, greed and cruelty we will gradually become a less viable species of human being.

As individuals we can only live our own lives and engage in whatever conversations we think will be most helpful. My attitude today is to believe in love and try to practice it. Penelope and I have enjoyed our married life for over 30 years. I'm glad to say that Alastair and Rachael (and even Fred) seem to have quite happy lives today. Alastair takes great satisfaction from loving relationships and helping other people with their problems; he still eats more chocolate than I do! I trust there is joy and contentment in your life too. We are all dancing and singing along and our principal partner is an uncertainty in which we can trust because, whatever it is, it dances well.

There will always be more questions than answers as Rainer Maria Rilke explains in his *Letters to a Young Poet*: 'Be patient towards all that is unsolved in your heart and try to love the questions themselves . . . Do not now seek the answers, which cannot be given because you would not be able to live them. And the point is to live everything. Live the questions now. Perhaps you will . . . gradually, without noticing it, live along some distant day into the answer.'

# Coda

There are two aspects of our experience that I think happen only once – our birth and our death.

It is probably towards the end of our lives that we become most aware of the creative power of our own imagination. Though I have tried to live in love as much as possible, some fear of the unknown remains with me, tempered by an awe and wonder that I believe come from Nature herself.

My aim has been to fall in love with the unknown. The experience of dying will be a first time as was the experience of being born and I know as little about the latter as I did about the former. In honouring life – and my life in particular – I have to accept that death is as natural as being born, but I do have the opportunity to express my gratitude for all that I have experienced.

I came from the unknown and must return to it and I am incredibly thankful for my life.

That's my story about the mind. I wish it was a song so you could hear the tune as well as the words. On the other hand I realise that it's much better for you to sing it for yourself, in your own way.

# Acknowledgements

Everyone I've ever met could have been my teacher, but even the ones I am aware of are so many and varied I've lost count. Together with reading, which is a big part of my life, the conversations with friends and fellow-travellers on life's journey, with my students, colleagues and family, have all been catalysts for the telling of my story. What I have written here has grown from my interactions with other people wherever meaningful connections have been made. This happens whether you plan it or not. The words I use are a product of that interaction so without the words spoken and written by others I can't imagine what I would say.

The person whose science shaped my thinking most is Humberto Maturana Romesin whom I think of with affection and to whom I owe a special debt of gratitude. Stephen Porges studied stress with a broad biological brush (as I tried to do) and I appreciate his beautiful insights. Iain McGilchrist's brilliant work is an inspiration to me. Jaak Panksepp is an animal researcher as I was and his ability to see broad principles amongst all the detail has also helped me. From the words of the late John O'Donohue and Eckhart Tolle I felt that I was learning about spirituality and that it was a privilege to do so.

The following people were kind enough to read draft versions of this manuscript: Penelope Fell, Julian Horne, Col Jennings, Pat Jennings, James Jeffrey, Phill Buckmaster, Barry Dack, Terry Williams, Alan Stewart, Mandy Galbraith and Brad Cook. I thank them for their helpful comments.

My thanks also to lulu.com for making it possible to publish in this way.